Elementary Hindi

WORKBOOK

प्राथमिक हिन्दी अभ्यास-पुस्तक

An Introduction to the Language

RICHARD DELACY AND SUDHA JOSHI

TUTTLE Publishing

Tokyo | Rutland, Vermont | Singapore

"Books to Span the East and West"

Tuttle Publishing was founded in 1832 in the small New England town of Rutland, Vermont [USA]. Our core values remain as strong today as they were then—to publish best-in-class books which bring people together one page at a time. In 1948, we established a publishing outpost in Japan—and Tuttle is now a leader in publishing English-language books about the arts, languages and cultures of Asia. The world has become a much smaller place today and Asia's economic and cultural influence has grown. Yet the need for meaningful dialogue and information about this diverse region has never been greater. Over the past seven decades, Tuttle has published thousands of books on subjects ranging from martial arts and paper crafts to language learning and literature—and our talented authors, illustrators, designers and photographers have won many prestigious awards. We welcome you to explore the wealth of information available on Asia at www.tuttlepublishing.com. **www.tuttlepublishing.com**.

Published by Tuttle Publishing, an imprint of Periplus Editions (HK) Ltd.

www.tuttlepublishing.com

Copyright © 2009, 2014 by Richard Delacy and Sudha Joshi
Cover image © R. Gino Santa Maria | Dreamstime.com

ISBN 978-0-8048-4503-8

First edition
29 28 27 26 25 24   8 7 6 5 4   2402VP
Printed in Malaysia

Distributed by:

North America, Latin America & Europe
Tuttle Publishing, 364 Innovation Drive,
North Clarendon,
VT 05759-9436 U.S.A
Tel: 1 (802) 773 8930
Fax: 1 (802) 773 6993
info@tuttlepublishing.com
www.tuttlepublishing.com

Asia-Pacific
Berkeley Books Pte Ltd, 3 Kallang Sector #04-01,
Singapore 349278
Tel: (65) 6741-2178
Fax: (65) 6741-2179
inquiries@periplus.com.sg
www.tuttlepublishing.com

TUTTLE PUBLISHING® is a registered tradmark of Tuttle Publishing, a division of Periplus Editions (HK) Ltd.

Contents

Introduction

Elementary Hindi is aimed at those with no background in Hindi. For this reason it focuses on literacy as well as developing basic listening and speaking skills. The primary goal is to bring you, the learner, to a point where you possess the tools to go on to become fluent in Hindi.

How to Use This Book

Elementary Hindi is divided into a Textbook, an Online Audio, and a Workbook containing activities and conversations that closely follow the structure of the Textbook. Whether you are learning Hindi in a classroom setting or on your own, *Elementary Hindi* will help you learn the basics of the language.

The lessons in the **Textbook** are designed so that learners may complete a lesson a week over approximately 24 weeks. This represents a sufficient amount of time to integrate the material covered in each lesson. Each Textbook lesson contains explanations, examples of the grammatical concepts in practice, exercises and cultural information that will reinforce the material and make the learning process enjoyable. The Textbook's *Practice* exercises are in a format conducive to group work, so independent learners will want to approach these with an eye toward experiencing each facet of the exercises—creating the questions, then creating the answers, for example.

The **Online Audio** allows learners to hear all of the Textbook's Hindi passages and conversations, along with their questions and answers. It also includes the sounds and reading activities that are in the Workbook, and the Workbook's conversations, questions and answers. Throughout, the symbol 🎧 indicates the items that have corresponding audio.

The **Workbook** offers *Activities* that are designed for thorough practice of the concepts and vocabulary in each chapter, and its material should be completed as concepts are covered in the Textbook. The Workbook also contains a key to every activity so that learners can monitor their own progress. Activities are designed so that learners can understand with relative ease what is expected of them and may further consolidate their knowledge while taking control of their learning experience through self-correction. It is recommended that teachers assign the Workbook Activities to be completed outside of the class.

Modern Standard Hindi

Spoken Hindi possesses a tremendous variety of registers across the length and breadth of the north of India. All of these spoken forms vary to differing degrees and, depending on the individuals, are more or less mutually intelligible to speakers of other registers. Hindi's many spoken forms are generally included under the rubric of "Modern Standard Hindi," the codified written form of the language based on the spoken language that evolved in and around Delhi (kharī bolī) over two hundred years ago. This form of Hindi is employed as the medium of instruction in many schools at the primary and high school levels and used more or less in official discourse as well as in the various media across north India. It is also this form of Hindi that possesses, at a basic spoken level, a close relationship lexically and grammatically with Urdu, another major language of India and the national language of Pakistan, written in a modified form of the Arabic script.

Given its prominence, Modern Standard Hindi is presented in introductory books such as this one, with the view that knowledge of a basic standard form enables the student to go on to read literary texts, watch Hindi films and engage with various other forms of media. Learning this form of Hindi also allows the student to communicate effectively with the widest possible range of speakers across the Hindi-speaking region in the north, putting the student in a good position to begin to develop an appreciation for the nuances of any of Hindi's many different regional spoken registers.

LESSON 1 पहला पाठ

The Basic Sentence; Asking Questions

ACTIVITY 1.1

Listen to the online audio and repeat the sounds below in the pauses provided, focusing on your pronunciation of the consonants and vowels introduced in Lesson 1. Next, read the words below while listening to them on the online audio.

क/क़	न	प	म	य	ल	व	ह
अ	आ	ई	ऐ				
का/क़ा	ना	पा	मा	या	ला	वा	हा
की/क़ी	नी	पी	मी	यी	ली	वी	ही
कै/कै़	नै	पै	मै	यै	लै	वै	है

अली Ali (name)
आना to come (*v.i.*)
ऐ O!
कला art (*f*)
काला black
कै vomiting (*f*)
नाई barber (*m*)
नाना (maternal) grandfather (*m*)
नानी (maternal) grandmother (*f*)

नैना eye (*m pl*)
पा to obtain (*v.t.*)
पी drink, drank
पीना to drink (*v.t.*)
पानी water (*m*)
पैना sharp
माला garland (*f*)
माली gardener (*m*)
मामा (maternal) uncle (*m*)

मामी maternal aunt (*f*)
या or (*conj*)
यानी that is to say
लाई brought (*v.i.*)
वाला wallah
ही only, just
है is (*v.i.*)

ACTIVITY 1.2

See if you can read the following words, keeping in mind the rules of pronunciation. Then listen to the online audio and repeat them in the pauses provided.

अपना one's own
आप you
आम ordinary; mango (*m*)
आय income (*f*)
ईमान faith, belief, integrity (*m*)
ऐनक spectacles (*f*)
कई several
कम less
कमल lotus (*m*)
कल yesterday/tomorrow (*m*)
क़लम pen (*f*)
कहना to say (*v.t.*)

कहानी story (*f*)
कापी notebook (*f*)
काम work (*m*)
क्या what (*inter*)
नमक salt (*m*)
नहाना to bathe (*v.t.* + *v.i.*)
नाम name (*m*)
पकना to be cooked, to ripen (*v.i.*)
पक्का strong; ripe
पहनना to wear (*v.t.*)
मन heart/mind (*m*)
मनाना to persuade; appease (*v.t.*)

महल palace (*m*)
महीना month (*m*)
मानना to accept, agree (*v.t.*)
यह he/she, it, this
वन forest (*m*)
वह he/she, it, that
वाक्य sentence (*m*)
वाला wallah
है is (*v.i.*)

ACTIVITY 1.3

Translate the following sentences into English.

1. आम क्या है? _____

2. क्या यह आम है? _____

3. यह पीला आम है। _____

4. नमक क्या है? _____

5. क्या यह नमक है? _____

6. यह कम नमक है। _____

7. वह कहानी क्या है? _____

8. क्या वह कहानी है? _____

9. वह कहानी है। _____

10. कमल क्या है? _____

11. क्या वह लाल कमल है? _____

12. क्या वह कमल लाल है? _____

ACTIVITY 1.4

Translate the following sentences into Hindi. Then listen to the online audio, repeating these sentences in the pauses provided.

1. Is this a strong house? ....

2. This is a strong house. ....

3. What is this? ....

4. That is a notebook. ....

5. Is this the first month? ....

6. What is that? ....

7. This is a red pen. ....

8. Is that pen red? ....

9. This pen is red. ....

10. This water is blue. ....

11. Is this *pān*? ....

12. That is *pān*. ....

13. What is *pān*? ....

14. Is this too little work? ....

Glossary शब्दावली

The following words appear in the Activities that accompany Lesson 1. Most are common everyday words. Take a moment to study them along with the genders of the nouns.

आम mango (*m*); ordinary	नमक salt (*m*)	महल palace (*m*)
कम less, too little	नया new	महीना month (*m*)
कमल lotus (*m*)	नीला blue	यह he/she, this, it (close to the speaker)
क़लम pen (*f*)	पक्का ripe, strong	लाल red
कहानी story (*f*)	पहला first	वन forest (*m*)
कान ear (*m*)	पान betel leaf (*m*)	वह he/she, that, it (far from the speaker)
कापी notebook (*f*)	पानी water (*m*)	वाक्य sentence (*m*)
काम work (*m*)	पीला yellow	है is (*v.i.*)
क्या what? (*and question marker*)	मकान house (*m*)	

LESSON 2 दूसरा पाठ

Greetings; Introductions

ACTIVITY 2.1

Listen to the online audio and repeat the sounds below in the pauses provided, focusing on your pronunciation of the consonants and vowels. Next, read the words below while listening to them on the online audio.

ज/ज़	त	द	ब	र	स
इ	उ	ए			
जि/ज़ि	ति	दि	बि	रि	सि
जु/ज़ु	तु	दु	बु	रु	सु
जे/ज़े	ते	दे	बे	रे	से
हाँ	नहीं	हैं			

अलमारी cupboard (f)
आज today (m)
आदमी man (m)
आसान easy
इमारत building (f)
ईद the festival of Eid (f)
उतरना to descend (v.i.)
उदास sad
एक one
ऐसा such
कमरा room (m)
किताब book (f)
क़ीमत price (f)
क़मीज़ shirt (f)
ज़बान tongue, language (f)
जी हाँ yes

जीवन life (m)
तारा star (m)
दाँत tooth (m)
दाम price (m)
दाल lentils (f)
दुआ prayer (f)
देना to give (v.t.)
नमस्ते greeting and goodbye
नहीं no
पता address, whereabouts (m)
पैसा paisa, money (m)
बहन sister (f)
बाज़ार market (m)
बुलाना to call (v.t.)
में in
मैं I

मिलना to meet (v.i.)
यहाँ here
ये he/she/they/these
रुई cotton (f)
रुपया a rupee (m)
रविवार Sunday (m)
वहाँ there
वे he/she/they/those
समय time (m)
सस्ता cheap
साहब sahib (m)
हँसना to laugh (v.i.)
हाँ yes
हैं are (v.i.)

ACTIVITY 2.2

Translate the following sentences into English.

1. यह हमारा कमरा है । _____

2. आपका कमरा कहाँ है? _____

3. क्या वह सितार सस्ता है? _____

4. जी हाँ, यह सितार सस्ता है । _____

5. मेरा एक सवाल है । _____

6. आपका सवाल क्या है? _____

7. एक कलम का दाम क्या है? _____

8. एक कलम का दाम एक पैसा है । _____

9. क्या यह नया बाज़ार है? _____

10. जी नहीं, यह लाल बाज़ार है । _____

ACTIVITY 2.3

Translate the following sentences into Hindi. Then listen to the online audio and repeat these sentences in the pauses provided.

1. My name is Deepak. _____

2. What is your name? _____

3. My name is Kavita. _____

4. What is the price of the book? _____

5. Where is your sister? _____

6. Is his house new? _____

7. Yes, his house is new. _____

8. Is this my shirt? _____

9. No, that is your sister's shirt. _____

10. Is this a man's voice? _____

11. What is your address? _____

12. No, my sister is not here. _____
    (Both *no* and *not* are expressed using नहीं in Hindi. The regular position for नहीं is directly before the verb.)

ACTIVITY 2.4

Following the example, answer the questions below substituting the correct form of the pronoun with the possessive postposition का indicated in the parentheses. Then listen to the online audio and answer the questions in the pauses provided.

Example:

क्या यह मेरा मकान है?   जी हाँ, वह आपका मकान है।

[Is this my house?]   *[Yes, that is your house.]*

1. क्या वह हमारी किताब है? जी नहीं, वह _____ किताब है। (his [singular form])

2. क्या ये आपके माँ-बाप हैं? जी हाँ, ये _____ माँ-बाप हैं। (my)

3. क्या यह इसकी क़मीज़ है? जी नहीं, यह _____ क़मीज़ है। (your)

4. क्या यह इनका कमरा है? जी हाँ, यह _____ कमरा है। (her)

5. क्या वे मेरे सितार हैं? जी नहीं, वे _____ सितार नहीं हैं। (your)

6. क्या वह इनका सामान है? जी हाँ, यह _____ सामान है। (their)

7. क्या वह हमारी दवा है? जी नहीं, यह _____ दवा है। (their)

ACTIVITY 2.5

Conversation बातचीत

🎧 Read and translate this conversation into English and then listen to it on the online audio. This is a conversation between two university students, Deepak and Kavita, and Kavita's mother, Sunita, in Khan Market in New Delhi. Deepak and Kavita study together at Delhi University. Deepak thinks that he recognizes Kavita's mother and begins talking to her.

Place   : Khan Market, New Delhi
Characters : Deepak, Kavita, Kavita's mother Sunita

दीपक	– नमस्ते, जी। क्या आप कविता की माँ हैं?
सुनीता	– जी हाँ। आप का नाम क्या है?
दीपक	– जी, मेरा नाम दीपक है।
सुनीता	– क्या आप का मकान यहाँ है?
दीपक	– जी नहीं, हमारा मकान यहाँ नहीं है। मेरे माँ-बाप इलाहाबाद में हैं। लेकिन यहाँ मेरे एक मामा जी हैं।
सुनीता	– आपके मामा जी का मकान कहाँ है?
दीपक	– वह सामने है।
कविता	– दीपक, नमस्ते। माँ, ये दीपक हैं।
दीपक	– नमस्ते कविता।
कविता	– दीपक, आपकी बहन कहाँ है?
दीपक	– आजकल वह इलाहाबाद में है। कविता, क्या यह आपकी किताब है?
कविता	– जी हाँ, यह मेरी किताब है।
दीपक	– इसका दाम क्या है?
कविता	– इसका दाम तीस रुपये है।
दीपक	– क्या यह कहानी की किताब है?
कविता	– जी हाँ, यह कहानी की किताब है।

सितार
sitar (m)

_____

🎧 Translate the following questions into Hindi based on the conversation. Then answer them in Hindi. Listen to the online audio and answer these questions in the pauses provided.

1. What is Kavita's mother's name? _____

2. What is your name? _____

3. Where are Deepak's parents? _____

4. Is Deepak's house in Allahabad? _____

5. Where is Deepak's sister these days? _____

6. What is the price of Kavita's book? _____

Glossary शब्दावली

The following words appear in the Activities that accompany Lesson 2. Most are common everyday words. Take a moment to study them along with the genders of the nouns.

आजकल these days
आदमी man (*m*)
आवाज़ voice, noise (*f*)
इलाहाबाद Allahabad (*m*)
इलाहाबाद में in Allahabad
एक one
कमरा room (*m*)
क़मीज़ shirt (*f*)
कविता Kavita (name)
कहाँ where (*inter*)
किताब book (*f*)
क़ीमत price (*f*)
जी heart, a term of respect placed after names

तीस thirty
दवा medicine (*f*)
दाम price (*m*)
दीपक Deepak (name)
नमस्ते greeting and goodbye
नाम name (*m*)
पता address, whereabouts (*m*)
पैसा *paisa*, money (*m*)
बहन sister (*f*)
बाज़ार market (*m*)
माँ mother (*f*)
माँ-बाप parents (*m pl*)
मामा uncle (*m*)

में in*
यहाँ here
रुपये rupees (*m pl*)
सवाल question (*m*)
सस्ता cheap
सामने in front
सामान luggage (*m*)
सितार sitar (*m*)
सुनीता Sunita (name)
हैं are (plural of the verb *to be*) (*v.i.*)

* Words such as में *in* are placed *after* the noun that they govern.

LESSON 3 तीसरा पाठ

Introducing Kavita

ACTIVITY 3.1

Listen to the online audio and repeat the sounds below in the pauses provided, focusing on your pronunciation of the consonants and vowels. Next, read the words below while listening to them on the online audio.

ख/ख़	घ	च	ड़	ध	
ऊ	ओ	औ			
खू/ख़ू	घू	चू	डू़	धू	रू
खो/ख़ो	घो	चो	ड़ो	धो	
खौ/ख़ौ	घौ	चौ	ड़ौ	धौ	

पकौड़ा a fried spicy food (m)

धोती dhoti (f)

अख़बार newspaper (m)	खाना food (m), to eat (v.t.)	पकौड़ा a fried spicy food (m)
अमरूद guava (m)	खोलना to open (v.t.)	पुल a bridge (m)
आँख eye (f)	घड़ी watch (f)	पूजा worship (f)
आँधी storm (f)	घर home (m)	बोलना to speak (v.t. + v.i.)
आलू potato (m)	घूमना to wander (v.i.)	मोज़ा sock (m)
ऊँचा high	चलना to move (v.i.)	मौसम weather (m)
ओर direction (f)	चाँदनी moonlight (f)	रसोई kitchen (f)
और and, more	चाय tea (f)	रोज़ day (m), daily
औरत woman (f)	चिड़िया bird (f)	लड़का boy (m)
ककड़ी cucumber (f)	चूड़ी bangle (f)	लड़की girl (f)
कपड़ा cloth (m)	चौंकना to be startled (v.i.)	साड़ी sari (f)
कूड़ा rubbish, trash (m)	ज़रूर certainly	समोसा samosa (m)
कोई someone, anyone	जूता shoe (m)	सुख happiness (m)
कौन who (inter)	तारीख़ date (f)	सुबह morning (f)
खड़ा standing	दूध milk (m)	सोचना to think (v.t.)
ख़त letter (m)	धोती dhoti (f)	हूँ am (v.i.)
ख़रीदना to buy (v.t.)	नौकरी job, employment (f)	होना to be (v.i.)

ACTIVITY 3.2

🎧 Fill in the blanks with the correct form of the adjective given in parentheses and then translate the following sentences into English. Then listen to the online audio and answer the questions in Hindi in the pauses provided.

1. आज का मौसम _____ है? (how) _____

2. आज का मौसम _____ है। (bad) _____

3. क्या यह _____ दवा है? (cheap) _____

4. जी हाँ, यह दवा _____ है। (cheap) _____

5. क्या ये आपके _____ आम हैं? (yellow) _____

6. जी हाँ, ये मेरे _____ आम हैं। (yellow) _____

7. बाहर _____ आदमी खड़े हैं? (how many) _____

8. बाहर _____ आदमी खड़े हैं। (five) _____

9. क्या आपकी किताब _____ है? (easy) _____

10. जी हाँ, मेरी किताब _____ है। (easy) _____

11. क्या वह _____ तरकारी है? (fresh) _____

12. जी नहीं, वह _____ तरकारी है। (stale) _____

13. क्या आप _____ हैं? (free) _____

14. जी नहीं, मैं _____ नहीं हूँ। (free) _____

15. यह _____ दीवार ख़राब है क्या? (entire)*
    * Here the regular position of **क्या** should be understood as being at the beginning of the sentence.

16. जी हाँ, वह _____ है। (bad) _____

17. वह लड़की _____ है? (how) _____

18. वह लड़की बहुत _____ है। (beautiful) _____

ACTIVITY 3.3

Translate the sentences into Hindi.

1. This boy is very big. _____

2. She is a very big girl. _____

3. What is today's date? _____

4. Today is the second. (*today two date is*) _____

5. Three men are standing* over there. _____
   * In Hindi there is no verb *to stand*. The adjective **खड़ा** *standing* is combined with the verb *to be* **होना**, resulting in **खड़ा होना** *to stand* (*to be standing*).

6. There are four fresh potatoes over there. (*four fresh potatoes over there are*) _____

7. The bottle of medicine is blue. (*medicine's bottle*) _____

8. Her sari is red. _____

ACTIVITY 3.4

Conversation बातचीत

Read and translate this conversation into English and then listen to it on the online audio.

Place   : Deepak's uncle's house, New Delhi
Characters : Deepak, Kavita

कविता - नमस्ते दीपक। आप कैसे हैं?

दीपक - नमस्ते कविता। मैं मज़े में हूँ। आपका क्या हाल है?

कविता - बस। आज का मौसम कितना ख़राब है!

दीपक - नहीं जी, आज मौसम इतना ख़राब नहीं।[1]

कविता - दीपक, आज का मौसम बहुत ख़राब है।

दीपक - आज तारीख़ क्या है, कविता जी?

कविता - आज दो तारीख़ है।

दीपक - क्या आप ख़ाली हैं?

कविता - हाँ दीपक, मैं ख़ाली हूँ। क्या काम है?[2]

दीपक - ज़रा हिन्दी[3] का काम है।

कविता - तो आपकी हिन्दी की किताब कहाँ है?

दीपक - वह बड़ी मेज़ पर है।

कविता - मेज़ पर दवा की एक नीली बोतल है, किताब नहीं।

कविता - वहाँ नहीं। यहाँ।

दीपक - ओ, हाँ। यह आपकी किताब है।

1. Often the verb *to be* in the simple present tense (here है) is omitted when there is a negative adverb.

2. The regular position of **क्या** *what* in this sentence is directly before the verb.

3. हिन्दी **hindī** = *Hindi*

Translate the following questions into Hindi. Then listen to the online audio and answer these questions in Hindi in the pauses provided.

1. How is Deepak today? _____

2. Is Kavita in good spirits? _____

3. How are you (what is your state) today? _____

4. Are you free today? _____

5. Is today's weather very bad? _____

6. What is on the big table? _____

7. Is there a blue bottle on the big table? _____

Glossary शब्दावली

The following words have appeared in the Activities that accompany Lesson 3. Most are common everyday words. Take a moment to study them along with the genders of the nouns.

आज today (*m*)
आलू potato (*m*)
आसान easy
इतना this much, so much
ओ O!
कितना how much, how many
कैसा how, what kind of
खड़ा standing
ख़राब bad
ख़ाली empty, free
ख़ूबसूरत beautiful
चार four
ज़रा a little
तरकारी vegetable (*f*)

ताज़ा fresh
तारीख़ date (*f*)
तीन three
तो so, then
दीवार wall (*f*)
दो two
पर on
पाँच five
पूरा complete
बड़ा big
बस okay, enough
बहुत very, a lot, much
बासी stale
बाहर outside

बोतल bottle (*f*)
मज़े में at perfect ease
मेज़ table (*f*)
मेज़ पर on the table
मौसम weather (*m*)
यहाँ (over) here
लड़का boy (*m*)
लड़की girl (*f*)
वहाँ (over) there
साड़ी sari (*f*)
सारा entire
हाँ yes
हाल condition, state (*m*)
हूँ am (used with मैं *I*) (*v.i.*)

LESSON 4 चौथा पाठ

More about Deepak

ACTIVITY 4.1

🎧 Listen to the online audio and repeat the sounds below in the pauses provided, focusing on your pronunciation of the consonants and vowels introduced in Lesson 4. Next, read the words below while listening to them on the online audio.

ग/ग़	ड	ढ़	फ/फ़									
ऋ												
कृ	ग्र	घृ	तृ	द्र	धृ	नृ	पृ	बृ	मृ	वृ	सृ	ह्
क	का	कि	की	कु	कू	कृ	के	कै	को	कौ		

अगर if (*conj*)
अफ़सर officer (*m*)
ऋतु season (*f*)
कागज़ paper (*m*)
काफ़ी enough
कृपा mercy (*f*)
गला throat (*m*)
ग़रीब poor

गुसलख़ाना bathroom (*m*)
चढ़ना to climb (*v.i.*)
चिढ़ाना to tease (*v.t.*)
डाक mail (*f*)
डाकू bandit (*m*)
तुम्हारा your
फल fruit (*m*)
फ़ुरसत free time, leisure (*f*)

फूल flower (*m*)
बढ़ना to increase, grow (*v.i.*)
माँगना to demand (*v.t.*)
मृदु soft
लिफ़ाफ़ा envelope (*m*)
लोग people (*m*)
हृदय heart (*m*)

ACTIVITY 4.2

Fill in the blanks in the following sentences with the correct form of the verb होना *to be* and then translate the sentences into English.

1. नमस्ते जी, आप कैसे ....?

....

2. नमस्कार जी, आप कैसी ....?

....

3. आप का नाम क्या ....?

....

4. मेरा नाम दीपक _____ ।

_____

5. और तू कौन _____ ?

_____

6. जी,* मैं कविता _____ ।
   * Here जी is a polite vocative particle.

_____

7. दीपक, आजकल तुम्हारी बहन कहाँ _____ ?

_____

8. क्या तुम आजकल इलाहाबाद में _____ ?

_____

9. इनके दोस्त यहाँ नहीं _____ ।

_____

10. किसका दोस्त वहाँ _____ ?

_____

11. यहाँ कितने मकान _____ ?

_____

12. अब किसकी बारी _____ ?

_____

13. उस की बारी _____ ।

_____

ACTIVITY 4.3

🎧 Translate these sentences into Hindi. Then listen to the online audio and repeat them in the pauses provided.

1. My blue shirt is on the table. ⸻

2. Your book('s) shop is very big. (Use the possessive form of तुम) ⸻

3. How many old newspapers are on the table? ⸻

4. There are five old newspapers on the table. ⸻

5. Our tea is fresh. ⸻

6. Is there enough sugar in your (Use the possessive form of आप) tea? ⸻

7. Yesterday's milk is off (bad). ⸻

8. Whose are these beautiful flowers? ⸻

9. Your watch is quite new. ⸻

10. Someone's glass('s) bangle is on the table. ⸻

ACTIVITY 4.4

Conversation बातचीत
🎧 Read and translate this conversation into English and then listen to it on the online audio. Here Deepak and his uncle attend a party at Kavita's friend Juhi's house. Deepak gives Kavita some flowers.

Place　　　 : Juhi's house
Characters : Deepak, Kavita, Juhi

जुही　 – नमस्ते जी, आपका नाम क्या है?
दीपक　 – जी, मैं दीपक हूँ। और आप कौन हैं?
जुही　 – मैं जुही हूँ। कविता कहाँ है?
दीपक　 – कविता बाहर है।
जुही　 – वहाँ कौन खड़ा है?

दीपक -	वे मेरे मामा जी हैं।[1]
जुही -	उनका नाम क्या है?
दीपक -	उनका नाम कृपा लाल है। कविता का परिवार कहाँ है?
जुही -	उसकी माँ बाहर खड़ी हैं। अरे कविता, यहाँ आओ। तुम्हारे पिताजी कहाँ हैं?
कविता -	हाय जुही, मेरे पिता जी बाहर खड़े हैं। अरे दीपक, तुम कैसे हो?
दीपक -	मेहरबानी है। तुम्हारा क्या हाल है?
कविता -	आज मेरा गला ज़रा ख़राब है। जुही, तुम्हारा मकान बहुत ख़ूबसूरत है। लेकिन आज बहुत लोग हैं यहाँ।
जुही -	हाँ, ये सब लोग पिता जी के दोस्त हैं।
दीपक -	कविता, ये फूल तुम्हारे लिये हैं।
कविता -	ये बहुत ख़ूबसूरत हैं।
जुही -	यह क्या बात है?
दीपक -	ऐसी कोई बात नहीं।

1. In some of the sentences plural pronouns (वे, उनका) have been used, adjectives declined in the plural (मेरे, खड़े) and corresponding verbs conjugated in the plural to indicate respect. Respect is also conveyed through the use of the honorific suffix जी (see Textbook p. 15).

 Translate the following questions into Hindi. Then listen to the online audio and answer these questions in the pauses provided.

1. What is Kavita's friend's name? ....

2. Where is Kavita's mother standing? ....

3. Is Juhi's house very beautiful? ....

4. Is Kavita's throat sore (bad) today? ....

5. For whom are the flowers? ....

6. Is Juhi Kavita's friend? ....

Glossary शब्दावली

The words below have appeared in the Activities that accompany Lesson 4. Most are common everyday words. Take a moment to study them along with the genders of the nouns.

अख़बार newspaper (*m*)

अब now

अरे hey!

आओ come (*imperative*)

ऐसा such, of this type

ऐसी कोई बात नहीं it's nothing (no such matter)

काँच glass (*m*)

काफ़ी enough

किसका whose (*inter*)

किसके लिये for whom (*inter*)

कोई some, any

कौन who (*inter*)

ख़त letter (*m*)

गला throat (*m*)

घड़ी watch (*f*)

चाय tea (*f*)

चीनी sugar (*f*)

चूड़ी bangle (*f*)

तुम्हारे लिये for you

दुकान shop (*f*)

दूध milk (*m*)

दोस्त friend (*m/f*)

नमस्कार greeting (*m*)

परिवार family (*m*)

पिता father (*m*)

पुराना old (said of things)

फूल flower (*m*)

बात matter, talk, thing (*f*)

बारी turn (as in *whose turn?*) (*f*)

मेहरबानी kindness, favor (*f*)

 (here: thanks for asking)

लेकिन but (*conj*)

लोग people (*m*)

हाय hi!

Kavita's Family

🎧 Listen to the online audio and repeat the sounds below in the pauses provided, focusing on your pronunciation of the consonants introduced in Lesson 5. See if you can read the words below and then listen to them on the online audio.

छ	ठ	थ	भ	श

अच्छा good
अस्पताल hospital (*m*)
अतः therefore
अवश्य necessarily, certainly
असम्भव impossible
आवश्यक necessary
आशा hope (*f*)
ईश्वर/ईश्र god (*m*)
उठना to arise, to awake (*v.i.*)
कच्चा raw, unripe, unfinished
कठिन hard, difficult
कभी at any time, ever
ख़ुशी happiness (*f*)
गुरु teacher (*m*), heavy
गोश्त meat (*m*)

चश्मा eye glasses (*m*)
छतरी umbrella (*f*)
ज़रूर certainly
ठीक okay, correct
दया mercy, pity, compassion (*f*)
देश country (*m*)
नाश्ता refreshment, breakfast (*m*)
बस्ता school bag, satchel (*m*)
बीमार sick
बृहस्पतिवार Thursday (*m*)
भाई brother (*m*)
भारत India (*m*)
भूलना to forget (*v.i.*)
मच्छर mosquito (*m*)
लस्सी lassi (*f*)

लाठी stick (*f*)
शनिवार Saturday (*m*)
शरबत sherbert (*m*)
शराब wine, alcohol (*f*)
शहर city (*m*)
शाम evening (*f*)
शायद perhaps
शिव Shiva (*m*), auspicious
शीशा mirror (*m*)
शुभ auspicious, good (*m*)
शुरू beginning (*m*)
सच्चा true
सेठ wealthy merchant (*m*)
स्वागत welcome (*m*)

Fill in the blanks with the correct form of the verb होना *to be* in the simple past tense and then translate these sentences into English.

1. उसकी किताब वहाँ .... ।

   ....

2. कल आप कहाँ .... ? (*f*)

   ....

3. आपके पिता जी घर में .... ।

4. वह यहाँ नहीं .... । (*m*)

5. तुम स्कूल में क्यों नहीं .... ? (*f*)

6. कल मैं कॉलेज में .... । (*m*)

7. वह बिलकुल बेवफ़ा .... । (*m*)

8. कल सोमवार .... ।

9. इनके दोस्त यहाँ नहीं .... ।

10. कल मौसम कैसा .... ?

11. यहाँ कितने खूबसूरत मकान .... ?

12. कलम का दाम क्या .... ?

ACTIVITY 5.3

Translate these sentences into Hindi (using the appropriate form of either कैसा or कितना) and then listen to the online audio and answer the questions in the pauses provided.

1. How high is this wall? This wall is very high.

2. How are you today? (तुम) I am okay today.

3. How many newspapers were here? There were several newspapers here.

4. What sort of newspaper is that? That newspaper is good.

5. How is that newspaper? It is not very good.

6. What sort of shop was that? It was a very big shop.

7. How many people are *in the world*? What a stupid('s) question.

8. How was that man? That man was unfaithful.

9. How beautiful were those flowers! Yes, very.

10. What sort of work was it? (वह) (It) was good work.

ACTIVITY 5.4

Conversation बातचीत

Read and translate this conversation into English and then listen to it on the online audio. Here Deepak and Kavita meet at Delhi University.

Place   : Delhi University
Characters : Deepak, Kavita

दीपक — नमस्ते कविता, तुम कैसी हो?

कविता — हाय दीपक! मैं बिलकुल ठीक हूँ। तुम्हारा क्या हाल है?

दीपक — बस, मेरा हाल अच्छा है। कल तुम कहाँ थीं, कविता?[1]

कविता — कल मैं घर में थी, मैं बीमार थी। आज कितना अच्छा दिन है!

दीपक — हाँ, बहुत अच्छा है। ओह, यह कैसी किताब है?

कविता — बहुत अच्छी तो नहीं लेकिन ठीक है।

दीपक — आज तुम्हारे दोस्त कहाँ हैं?

कविता — आज वे कॉलेज[2] में नहीं हैं।

दीपक — आज तुम्हारे कितने क्लास हैं?

कविता — आज चार क्लास हैं मेरे।

दीपक — वहाँ किताब की दुकान में कितने लोग खड़े हैं?

कविता — तीन लोग हैं। वह कैसी दुकान है?

दीपक — दुकान तो[3] अच्छी है।

कविता — अच्छा दीपक, नमस्ते।

दीपक — नमस्ते कविता।

1. Here the word order has been changed to emphasize the word थीं *were*.

2. The symbol ˘ above the vowel आ in the word कॉलेज *college* marks the presence of the English sound /o/ as in John, college, Boston, etc. For example, जान = *life (f)* whereas जॉन = *John*.

3. Here तो is used as an emphatic particle and is not easily translated into English.

_____

_____

_____

_____

_____

Translate the following questions into Hindi, and answer them in Hindi based on the conversation. Listen to the online audio and answer these questions in the pauses provided.

1. Is Kavita absolutely fine today? _____

2. Where was Kavita yesterday? _____

3. Was Kavita sick yesterday? _____

4. Were you sick yesterday? _____

5. Was your brother/sister sick yesterday?* _____
   * If you don't have a brother, you can say मेरा भाई नहीं है। If you don't have a sister, you can say मेरी बहन नहीं है।

6. Is today's weather good? _____

7. How many people are standing in the shop? _____

8. How is the shop? _____

Glossary शब्दावली

The following words have appeared in the Activities that accompany Lesson 5. Most are common everyday words. Take a moment to study them along with the genders of the nouns.

ऊँचा high	घर में at home	बेकार useless, stupid
ओह oh!	ठीक okay	बेवफ़ा unfaithful[1]
कई several	तो then, so, emphatic particle	सोमवार Monday (m)
कल yesterday, tomorrow (m)	दिन day (m)	स्कूल school (m)
कॉलेज college (m)	दुनिया में in the world	ही only, just[2]
कैसा what sort of, how	बिलकुल absolutely	
क्लास class (m/f)	बीमार sick, ill	

1. बेवफ़ा *unfaithful* is an indeclinable adjective. In other words, it does not change for the noun or pronoun that it qualifies.
2. ही follows the word that is emphasized and can never stand alone.

LESSON **6** छठा पाठ

Meeting Deepak's Family

Listen to the online audio and repeat the sounds below in the pauses provided, focusing on your pronunciation of the consonants introduced in Lesson 6. See if you can read the words below and then listen to them on the online audio.

ङ	झ/भ	ञ	ट	ढ	ण/ग	ष

अंगूठी ring (f)

अंगूर grape (m)

अंग्रेज़ी English language (f)

अण्डा egg (m)

अंधेरा darkness (m), dark

अद्भुत marvelous

आज्ञा order, command (f)

आटा wholemeal flour (m)

आश्रम hermitage (m)

इकट्ठा collected (adj)

उत्तर answer, north (m)

ऋषि sage (m)

कंघी comb (f)

कक्षा class (f)

कष्ट suffering (m)

कारण reason (m)

कुत्ता dog (m)

क्रोध anger (m)

क्षमा forgiveness (f)

गंगा Ganges (f)

गर्मी heat (f)

घंटा bell, an hour (m)

घमण्ड vanity, arrogance (m)

चंद्र moon (m)

चिट्ठी letter (f)

चिह्न a sign (m)

छोटा small

जंगल forest (m)

जंगली savage

जिह्वा tongue (f)

ज्ञान knowledge (m)

झण्डा flag (m)

झाँकना to peep (v.t.)

झुंड herd, flock (m)

झूठ lie (m)

झोंपड़ी hut (f)

झोला bag (m)

टमाटर tomato (m)

टहलना to stroll (v.i.)

टाँगना to hang (v.t.)

टिकट ticket (m/f)

टुकड़ा piece (m)

टूटना to break (v.i.)

टोपी cap (f)

ठंड cold (f)

डण्डा stick (m)

ढूँढना to search (v.t.)

ढेर heap, pile (m)

तंग tight

तिथि date (f)

तीर्थ holy place (m)

थकना to become tired (v.i.)

थाली a metal plate (f)

थोड़ा a little

दक्षिण south (m)

दफ़्तर office (m)

दर्शन appearance, sight, philosophy (m)

दीक्षा initiation (f)

दुष्ट wicked

द्वारा by means of

निमंत्रण invitation (m)

निर्बल weak

पंच five, an arbitrator

पंजा claw (m)

पंडित pandit (m)

पत्र letter (m)

परीक्षा examination (f)

पर्यटन touring, tourism (m)

पुरुष man (m)

पूर्व the east (m), former

पृथ्वी the earth (f)

पृष्ठ page (m)

पेट stomach (m)

प्रणाम respectful greeting, salutation (m)

प्रतिदिन every day

प्रतीक्षा waiting (f)

प्रयत्न effort (m)

प्रशंसा praise (f)

प्रश्न question (m)

प्रसन्नता happiness (f)

प्रसिद्ध famous

प्राण life (m)

प्रार्थना prayer (f)

प्रेम love (m)

फ़र्श floor (m)

फ़ुर्सत leisure (f)

बुद्धू idiot

ब्रह्मा Brahma (m)

ब्राह्मण Brahman (m)
भक्त devotee (m)
भाषा language (f)
मंगलवार Tuesday (m)
मंत्री minister (m)
महर्षि great sage (m)
महाराष्ट्र the great nation (m)
मिट्टी soil (f)
मित्र friend (m)
मिर्च chilli (f)
मुन्ना child (affectionate) (m)
मुफ़्त free, gratis
यात्रा journey (f)
रोटी bread (f)
लक्ष्मी the goddess of wealth (f)
लूटना to steal (v.t.)
लेटना to lie (down) (v.i.)

लौटना to return (v.i.)
वर्ष year (m)
वर्षा rain (f)
विद्या knowledge (f)
विद्यार्थी seeker of knowledge, student (m)
विशेष special
विश्राम rest (m)
विषय subject (m)
विष्णु Vishnu (m)
वृक्ष tree (m)
व्याकरण grammar (m)
व्रत fast (m)
शक्ति strength, power (f)
शिष्य disciple (m)
शुक्रवार Friday (m)
शुद्ध pure

श्रृंगार physical decoration (m)
संगीत music (m)
संस्कृत Sanskrit (f)
समझना to understand (v.t. + v.i.)
समझाना to explain (v.t.)
समृद्ध prosperous
सर्दी cold (f)
साथी friend, companion (m)
साधारण ordinary
सायंकाल evening (m)
सिंह lion (m)
सूर्य sun (m)
स्वर्ग heaven (m)
हड्डी bone (f)
हफ़्ता week (m)
हर्ष joy (m)

ACTIVITY 6.2

Look up the following words in your dictionary to practice this skill. They all appear in M. Chaturvedi and B. Tiwari (eds.), *A Practical Hindi-English Dictionary* (Delhi: National Publishing House, 2005). Write the English meanings and parts of speech. You can also look them up in the index at the back of the Textbook.

1. अक्खड़ _____

2. संस्कृत _____

3. दुष्टात्मा _____

4. ऐंद्रिय _____

5. ऐतिह्य _____

6. मुद्रा _____

7. राष्ट्र _____

8. फ़र्श _____

9. व्यक्ति _____

10. उन्नति _____

11. शून्य _____

12. ऐश्वर्य _____

13. अंतर्मुखी _____

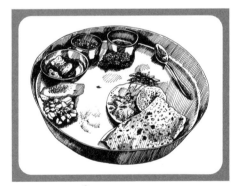

थाली a metal plate (f)

14. विज्ञान

15. अक्षर

16. पवित्र

ACTIVITY 6.3

Translate the following sentences into English and then listen to them on the online audio, repeating them in the pauses provided.

1. आज कौन-सा दिन है?

2. आज बुधवार है।

3. कल कौन-सा दिन था?

4. कल मंगलवार था।

5. कल सुबह आप कहाँ थीं?

6. कल सुबह मैं यहाँ नहीं थी।

7. कल रात तुम यहाँ क्यों नहीं थे?

8. कल रात मैं यहीं था।

9. यह कब की बात है?

10. यह बृहस्पतिवार की बात है।

ACTIVITY 6.4

Translate the following sentences into Hindi and then listen to them on the online audio, repeating them in the pauses provided.

1. Today is Saturday.

2. Yesterday was Friday.

3. Tomorrow is Sunday.

4. She has four brothers.

5. He has one sister.

6. This is the month of March.

ACTIVITY 6.5

Conversation बातचीत

Read and translate this conversation into English and then listen to it on the online audio. Here Kavita comes to Deepak's house to return a book.

स्थान (place)   : दीपक का घर
पात्र (characters) : दीपक, कविता

दीपक – अरे कविता, तुम यहाँ कैसे?[1] कल रात तुम कहाँ थीं?
कविता – कल मैं घर में ही[2] थी। क्यों?
दीपक – ऐसे ही। ओह यह मेरी हिन्दी की किताब है? यह कहाँ थी?
कविता – मेरी मेज़ पर थी।
दीपक – अच्छा, शुक्रिया। आओ, अंदर आओ। चाय या कॉफ़ी?
कविता – अभी कुछ नहीं, शुक्रिया। दीपक, तुम्हारे कितने भाई-बहन हैं?
दीपक – हम तीन भाई-बहन हैं। मेरे एक बड़े भाई और एक छोटी बहन है।
कविता – अभी सब लोग कहाँ हैं?
दीपक – बहन तो इलाहाबाद में है। और भाई यहीं हैं। तुम्हारे एक भाई हैं, न?[3]
कविता – जी हाँ, लेकिन आजकल वे ऑस्ट्रेलिया में हैं।
दीपक – वे ऑस्ट्रेलिया में कब से हैं?
कविता – वे दो साल से ऑस्ट्रेलिया में हैं।

1. Here कैसे may be translated as *for what reason*, and the whole phrase may be translated as *what brings you here?* In this sentence the verb *to come* has not been expressed. In this function the word कैसे is invariable and takes the masculine plural ending.
2. ही is an emphatic particle that may be translated as *just, only.*
3. When placed at the end of the sentence after the verb न is employed to make the rhetorical and seek confirmation from the listener. It may be translated as *isn't it?*

Translate the following questions into Hindi, then answer them in Hindi based on the conversation. Listen to the online audio and answer these questions in the pauses provided.

1. Where was Kavita last night? _____

2. Was Kavita just at home last night? _____

3. Where was Deepak's book? _____

4. How many brothers does Deepak have? (*Deepak's how many brothers are?*) _____

5. Is Deepak's brother older or younger? _____

6. How many brothers do you have? _____

7. Do you have a sister? _____

8. Is Kavita's brother in Australia? _____

9. For how long has he been there? (*since when is he there?*) _____

Glossary शब्दावली

The following words have appeared in the Activities that accompany Lesson 6. Most are common everyday words. Take a moment to study them along with the genders of the nouns.

अंदर inside
अभी right now
ऐसे ही no reason, just such
कब की बात when did this happen? (*when's matter*)
कब से since when, for how long
कॉफ़ी coffee (*f*)
कुछ some, something
कुछ नहीं nothing
कैसे how, in what manner
कौन-सा which (*inter*)
क्यों why (*inter*)
घर home (*m*)

छोटा small
तो so, then, an emphatic particle
देश country (*m*)
दो two
न no, not
पात्र character (*m*)
बुधवार Wednesday (*m*)
बृहस्पतिवार Thursday (*m*)
भाई brother (*m*)
भाई-बहन brothers and sisters, siblings (*m pl*)
मंगलवार Tuesday (*m*)
मार्च March (*m*)

यहीं right here
रविवार Sunday (*m*)*
रात night (*f*)
शनिवार Saturday (*m*)
शुक्रवार Friday (*m*)
शुक्रिया thank you (*m*)
सब all
साल year (*m*)
सुबह morning (*f*)
से since, from, by, with
स्थान place (*m*)
ही only, just (emphatic particle)

* There is an alternative word for Sunday, इतवार (*m*).

LESSON 7 सातवाँ पाठ

Some More Greetings; To Want/Need

Following the example, decline these masculine nouns for number and case. Write the meanings for each declension as well.

Singular Direct	Singular Oblique	Plural Direct	Plural Oblique
रुपया rupee	रुपये में in a/the rupee	रुपये rupees	रुपयों में in (the) rupees
दाम price (*m*)			
पेड़ tree (*m*)			
पिता father (*m*) (category 3)			
लड़का boy (*m*)			
कमरा room (*m*)			
आदमी man (*m*)			
फल fruit (*m*)			
मंत्री minister (*m*)			
लिफ़ाफ़ा envelope (*m*)			
पति husband (*m*)			
संवाददाता correspondent (*m*) (category 3)			
कुआँ water well (*m*)			
भालू bear (*m*)			
कीड़ा insect (*m*)			
राजा king (*m*) (category 3)			

ACTIVITY 7.2

🎧 Fill in the correct form of the noun in parentheses (declined appropriately for number and case) and then translate the sentences into English. Listen to them on the online audio and repeat them in the pauses provided.

1. आपका _____ क्या है? (address)

   _____

2. उन _____ का दाम क्या है? (sitars)

   _____

3. वहाँ कितने _____ खड़े हैं? (men)

   _____

4. एक सेब का दाम दस _____ है। (rupees)

   _____

5. इस _____ में कौन है? (room)

   _____

6. _____ किसको चाहिये? (*pān*)

   _____

7. उन _____ में से* कौन अच्छा है? (men)

   _____

   *में से from amongst

8. मेरे _____ में दर्द है। (throat)

   _____

9. तेरे कितने _____ हैं? (uncles)

   _____

10. _____ में कीड़े हैं। (potato)

    _____

ACTIVITY 7.3

🎧 Translate the following sentences into Hindi and then listen to them on the online audio and repeat them in the pauses provided.

1. This room is quite big.

2. Was there a bathroom with the big room?

3. How many rooms are empty?

4. There were four beds in some rooms.

5. What is the rent of this room?

6. My father has a headache. (*in my father's head pain is*)

7. Who are the owners of these two hotels? (*these two hotels' owners who are*)

8. There were three men in those two houses.

9. Where are the *dhobis* (washermen)?

10. How many brothers do you have? (*your how many brothers are*) (तुम)

ACTIVITY 7.4

🎧 Fill in the correct form of the pronoun given in the parentheses with the postposition को and then translate these sentences into English. Listen to them on the online audio and repeat them in the pauses provided.

1. _____ क्या चाहिये? (Use आप)

2. _____ कुछ नहीं चाहिये। (Use मैं)

3. कल _____ क्या चाहिये था? (Use वे)

4. कल _____ दो कमरे चाहिये थे। (Use यह)

5. अगले हफ़्ते _____ काम चाहिये? (Use कौन)

_____

6. अगले हफ़्ते _____ काम चाहिये। (Use हम)

_____

7. _____ धन नहीं चाहिये। (Use कोई)

_____

8. _____ पाँच संतरे चाहिये। (Use ये)

_____

9. क्या _____ उस कमरे में पलंग चाहिये? (Use तुम)

_____

10. _____ बढ़िया कपड़े चाहिये। (Use वह)

_____

ACTIVITY 7.5

Conversation बातचीत

🎧 Read and translate this conversation into English and then listen to it on the online audio. Here Kavita inquires about a hotel room for a friend of her father who is coming from America and is due to arrive in a week.

स्थान : होटल की लॉबी
पात्र : कविता, होटल का मालिक

कविता - नमस्कार जी, आप कैसे हैं?
मालिक - मैं बिल्कुल ठीक हूँ, आप सुनाओ।*

* सुनाओ *please relate (tell me how you are)*. This is the imperative form of the verb सुनाना *to relate, to tell*. The use of आप with सुनाओ is non-standard, as सुनाओ is the form of the imperative ordinarily used with तुम.

कविता – बस। अच्छी हूँ। जी, मुझे एक कमरा चाहिये।

मालिक – आपको कमरा किसके लिये चाहिये?

कविता – असल में यह कमरा मेरे लिये नहीं है। मेरे पिता जी के एक दोस्त को कमरा चाहिये।

मालिक – क्या आपके पिता जी के दोस्त इंडियन हैं?

कविता – जी नहीं वे भारत के नहीं हैं।[1] वे अमरीकी हैं। कमरा उनको अगले हफ़्ते चाहिये।

मालिक – अच्छा, तो उन्हें कितने दिन[2] के लिये कमरा चाहिये?

कविता – उनको पाँच दिन के लिये चाहिये। क्या हरेक कमरे के साथ गुसलख़ाना है?

मालिक – जी हाँ, दोनों सिंगल और डबल कमरों के साथ गुसलख़ाना है।

कविता – अच्छा, और इस होटल में गर्म पानी भी है, न?

मालिक – हाँ, हाँ, ज़रूर।

कविता – तो सिंगल कमरे का किराया कितना है?

मालिक – सिंगल कमरे का किराया डेढ़ हज़ार रुपये रोज़ है, और डबल कमरे का किराया ढाई हज़ार रुपये रोज़।

कविता – अच्छा, आसपास कितने और होटल हैं?

मालिक – शहर में बहुत सारे होटल हैं। क्यों?

कविता – ऐसे ही। अच्छा, कमरा कहाँ है?

मालिक – हाँ, हाँ इधर आओ।

1. वे भारत के नहीं हैं। *He is not from (of) India.* Some speakers employ से in place of का (for example, वे भारत से नहीं हैं।).
2. The word दिन *day* is occasionally used in the singular oblique where we would expect the plural oblique (दिनों). Often this is the case when it is preceded by a number, as in पाँच दिन के लिये *for five days*. This is the case with numerous other time words as well.

_____
_____
_____
_____
_____
_____
_____
_____
_____
_____
_____
_____
_____
_____
_____

🎧 Translate the following questions into Hindi, then answer them in Hindi based on the conversation. Listen to the online audio and answer these questions in the pauses provided.

1. What does Kavita want/need? ....

2. What do you want/need? (money, peace, tea, coffee) ....

3. For whom does Kavita want/need a room? ....

4. Is Kavita's father's friend Indian? ....

5. Are you Indian? ....

6. Are your parents Indian? ....

7. When does Kavita's father's friend want/need the room? ....

8. For how many days does he want/need the room? ....

9. What is the rent/price of a single room? ....

10. Are there many hotels in the city? ....

Glossary शब्दावली

The following words have appeared in the Activities that accompany Lesson 7. Most are common everyday words. Take a moment to study them along with the genders of the nouns.

अगले हफ़्ते next week
असल real, true
असल में in reality, actually
आसपास nearby
इधर here
ऐसे ही no reason
और and, more
कपड़ा cloth (m)
कहाँ का of where
कॉफ़ी coffee (f)
किराया rent (m)
किसके लिये for whom
कीड़ा insect (m)
कुआँ water well (m)
के साथ with
गर्म hot

गुसलखाना bathroom (m)
चाय tea (f)
ज़रूर certainly
डेढ़ one and a half
ढाई two and a half
दर्द pain (m)
धन wealth (m)
धोबी washerman (m)
पति husband (m)
पलंग bed (m)
पेड़ tree (m)
पैसा money (m pl)
फल fruit (m)
बढ़िया excellent
बहुत सारा very many
भालू bear (m)

मंत्री minister (m)
मालिक owner (m)
मालकिन owner (f)
में से amongst
राजा king (m)
रोज़ daily; day (m)
लॉबी lobby (f)
लिफ़ाफ़ा envelope (m)
शांति peace (f)
संतरा mandarin, orange (m)
संवाददाता correspondent (m)
सिर head (m)
सौ one hundred
हज़ार one thousand
हरेक each
होटल hotel (m)

LESSON **8** आठवाँ पाठ

How Many Siblings Do You Have?

ACTIVITY 8.1

Decline these feminine nouns for number and case following the example. Write the meanings for each declension as well.

Singular Direct	Singular Oblique	Plural Direct	Plural Oblique
लड़की (a/the) girl	लड़की के लिये for (a/the) girl	लड़कियाँ (the) girls	लड़कियों के लिये for (the) girls
भाषा language (f)			
वस्तु thing (f)			
चिड़िया bird (f)			
रस्सी rope (f)			
छत roof (f)			
आज्ञा order, command (f)			
गुड़िया doll (f)			
पत्नी wife (f)			
कविता poem (f)			
ख़बर news (f)			
छुट्टी holiday (f)			

ACTIVITY 8.2

🎧 Fill in the correct form of the noun in parentheses (declined for number and case) and then translate the sentences into English. Listen to them on the online audio and repeat them in the pauses provided.

1. इन _____ की माँ वहाँ खड़ी थीं। (girls)

   _____

2. आप की कितनी _____ हैं? (sisters)

   _____

3. क्या ये उन _____ के कपड़े हैं? (sisters)

   _____

4. इस बाज़ार में कितनी _____ थीं? (shops)

   _____

5. उस बाज़ार की _____ में अच्छा सामान नहीं है। (shops)

   _____

6. इस _____ का कपड़ा क्या है? (sari)

   _____

7. इन _____ में कुछ छेद हैं। (saris)

   _____

8. हिन्दुस्तान में कितनी _____ हैं? (languages)

   _____

9. क्या आपके मन में कोई _____ है? (desire)

   _____

10. जी हाँ, मेरे मन में बहुत _____ हैं। (desires)

    _____

ACTIVITY 8.3

🎧 Translate the following imperatives into English and repeat them on the online audio in the pauses provided. Write down the second person pronoun to which they relate.

Pronoun

1. मुझे क़लम दे।   इसे तस्वीर बेच।   यह किताब ले।

2. उसे गुड़ियाँ मत दो।   मुझको रस्सियाँ बेचो।   वह लाठी न लो।

3. हमें क़लमें दीजिये।   उनको मेज़ें न बेचिये।   एक समोसा लीजिए।

4. इन्हें घड़ियाँ दीजियेगा।   इसको दवाएँ बेचियेगा।   यह बोतलें लीजिएगा।

5. किसी को मिठाई देना।   हमें अच्छी चीज़ें बेचना।   इसकी भेंट को मत लेना।

ACTIVITY 8.4

Translate the following sentences into Hindi, paying particular attention to the use of postpositions (italicized in English). The nouns and pronouns underlined are to be declined in the oblique. (The numbers in the example indicate the order of the words in the Hindi sentence.)

```
7     6     5   1   2 3  4
Give  the pens  to these boys' sisters.
```

```
1    2     3    4    5     6     7
इन  लड़कों  की  बहनों  को  क़लमें  दीजिये।
```
(these boys' sisters to pens give)

1. This is my Hindi('s) book. _____

2. *In* this book there are twenty pages. _____

3. There are four books *on* the table. _____

4. *In* these four books there are some beautiful pictures. _____

5. That man's wife was standing *in* the courtyard. _____

6. Those men's wives were standing *in* the courtyard. _____

7. Give this book *to* <u>that man's wife</u>. ....

8. Give these books *to* <u>those men's wives</u>. ....

9. There is a beautiful poem *in* <u>that book</u>. ....

10. There are some beautiful poems *in* <u>this book</u>. ....

ACTIVITY 8.5

Conversation बातचीत

🎧 Read and translate this conversation into English and then listen to it on the online audio. Here Deepak, Kavita and Kavita's mother Sunita-*ji* are sitting in a café in New Delhi.

स्थान : नई दिल्ली में एक कॉफ़ी शॉप
पात्र : कविता, दीपक, कविता की माँ सुनीता

सुनीता – कविता, तुम सभी लोगों के लिये ऑर्डर दो।
कविता – ठीक है, माँ। दीपक, तुम्हें क्या चाहिये?
दीपक – मुझको चाय चाहिये। कविता तुम बताओ, तुम्हें क्या चाहिए?
कविता – मुझे सिर्फ़ कॉफ़ी चाहिये।
सुनीता – कविता, कुछ तो खाओ।
कविता – नहीं माँ, मुझे कुछ नहीं चाहिये।
दीपक – और जी, आप बताइए, आपको क्या चाहिये?
सुनीता – मुझे बस चाय चाहिये। ठीक है, कविता?
कविता – बिल्कुल। भाई-साहब! आप तैयार हैं? हमारा ऑर्डर लो।
वेटर – हाँ जी, फ़रमाइये।
दीपक – हमारे लिए दो कॉफ़ी और एक चाय लाओ।
कविता – दीपक, तुम मत बोलो। भाई-साहब, दो चाय और एक कॉफ़ी लाना।
सुनीता – दीपक! तुम कुछ खाना भी खाओ, तकल्लुफ़ मत करो।
कविता – माँ, ज़बरदस्ती मत करो!
दीपक – अच्छा, मेरे लिये दो समोसे लाओ।
कविता – तो हमें कितनी चीज़ें चाहिये? दो चाय, एक कॉफ़ी और दो समोसे।
किसी को कुछ और नहीं चाहिये? माँ, तुम्हें?
सुनीता – नहीं बेटा,* बस इतना काफ़ी है।
कविता – गर्म गर्म लाना, ठंडा कुछ मत लाना। समोसे ताज़े हैं, क्या?
वेटर – जी बिल्कुल।

* The word बेटा *son* is used here by Kavita's mother to refer to her daughter affectionately. It is also often not placed in the oblique for the vocative when used to refer to a girl.

_____

_____

_____

_____

_____

_____

_____

_____

_____

_____

_____

_____

_____

_____

_____

_____

_____

🎧 Translate the following questions based on the conversation and then take turns with a partner to ask and answer them. Listen to the online audio and answer these questions in Hindi in the pauses provided.

1. What does Deepak want? _____

2. Does Kavita only want tea? _____

3. What does everyone want? _____

4. How many samosas does Deepak want? _____

5. Are the samosas fresh? _____

6. Do you want tea right now? _____

Glossary शब्दावली

All of these words have appeared above in the Activities that accompany Lesson 8. Most are common everyday words. Take a moment to study them along with the genders of the nouns.

अभी right now

आँगन courtyard (*m*)

आज्ञा command, order (*f*)

ऑर्डर order (*m*)

इच्छा desire (*f*)

कविता poem (*f*)

कुछ something

कुछ और something more

के लिये for, in order to

ख़बर news (*f*)

खाना food (*m*)

खाना to eat (*v.t.*)

गुड़िया doll (*f*)

घड़ी watch (*f*)

चाट spicy fast food (*f*)

चिड़िया bird (*f*)

चित्र picture (*m*)

चीज़ thing (*f*)

छत roof, ceiling (*f*)

छुट्टी holiday (*f*)

छेद hole (*m*)

ज़बरदस्ती करना to force (*v.t.*)

ठंडा cold

तकल्लुफ़ formality (*m*)

तकल्लुफ़ करना to be formal (*v.t.*)

तस्वीर picture (*f*)

तैयार ready, prepared

तैयार होना to be prepared (*v.i.*)

देना to give (*v.t.*)

पत्नी wife (*f*)

पन्ना page (*m*)

फ़रमाना to request (*v.t.*)

बताना to tell (*v.t.*)

बीस twenty

बेचना to sell (*v.t.*)

बेटा son (sometimes used affectionately for girls)

बोलना to speak (*v.t. + v.i.*)

भाई-साहब sir (*m*)

भाषा language (*f*)

भी also (follows the word it includes)

भेंट gift (*f*)

मत don't (with imperative)

मन heart, mind (*m*)

मिठाई sweetmeat (*f*)

रस्सी rope (*f*)

लाठी stick (*f*)

लाना to bring (*v.i.*)

लेना to take (*v.t.*)

वस्तु thing (*f*)

सभी all

समोसा samosa (*m*)

सामान goods, luggage, stuff (*m*)

साहब Sir (*m*)

सिर्फ़ only, just

सुन्दर beautiful

हिन्दुस्तान India (*m*)

LESSON **9** नवाँ पाठ

What Do You Do?

🎧 Complete these sentences by filling in the blanks with the appropriate imperfect present tense form of the verbs given in parentheses. Then translate the sentences and listen to them on the online audio, repeating them in the pauses provided.

1. मैं (m) हिन्दी .... l (to study)

   ....

2. हम (f) रोज़ अख़बार .... l (to read)

   ....

3. वह (m) पत्र .... l (to write)

   ....

4. वे (f) बहुत काम नहीं .... l (to do)

   ....

5. तुम (f) वहाँ क्यों नहीं .... ? (to go)

   ....

6. मैं (f) कभी-कभी फ़िल्में .... l (to watch)

   ....

7. यह (m) बहुत शराब .... l (to drink)

   ....

8. आप (m) स्कूल कब .... l (to arrive)

   ....

9. तू (m) अमरीका में .... l (to live)

   ....

10. हम *(m)* कुछ पैसा नहीं _____ । *(to give)*

11. आप *(f)* खाना कब _____ ? *(to eat)*

12. वह *(f)* किस कमरे में _____ ? *(to sleep)*

13. तुम *(m)* जल्दी क्यों _____ ? *(to arise)*

14. तू *(m)* फूल क्यों _____ *(to break)*

15. यह *(m)* क्यों नहीं _____ *(to think)*

16. ये *(f)* कुछ नहीं _____ । *(to say)*

17. वे *(m)* बहुत मेहनत _____ । *(to do)*

18. ये *(m)* हमेशा मेरी गाड़ी _____ । *(to take)*

ACTIVITY 9.2

🎧 Translate the following sentences, employing को where necessary. Then listen to the online audio and repeat them in the pauses provided.

1. I (*m*) sell books. ....

2. I (*f*) sell books to people. ....

3. They (*f*) eat jalebis.* ....
   * Jalebi is a particular fried sweet that is made from flour and yoghurt and dipped in syrup.

4. He knows those shopkeepers. ....

5. You (*f*) teach me Hindi.* ....
   * This is not an imperative.

6. We (*m*) study English. ....

7. She dresses the boy (in)* good clothes. ....
   * In this sentence, *in* is not expressed in Hindi.

8. You (*m*) serve me tea.* ....
   * This is not an imperative.

9. I (*f*) read it every day. ....

10. They (*m*) know your brothers. ....

ACTIVITY 9.3

🎧 Practice the days of the week and dates with the postposition को in the sentences below, translating the first 7 into Hindi and the rest into English. Then listen to them on the online audio and repeat them in the pauses provided.

1. Don't come to my house *on* Monday. ....

2. Do you (*m*) go to college *on* Tuesday? ....

3. I (*m*) study Hindi *on* Wednesday. ....

4. *On* Thursday I (*f*) teach students Hindi. ....

5. *On* Friday we have a holiday. ....

6. *On* Saturday we go to my friend's house. ....

7. We do nothing *on* Sunday. ....

8. एक तारीख़ को मुझे फ़ोन करना।

9. दो तारीख़ को मेरे यहाँ आइये।

10. तीन तारीख़ को विश्वविद्यालय मत जाना।

11. हर चार तारीख़ को मैं फ़्लैट का किराया देता हूँ।

12. उसका जन्मदिन पाँच तारीख़ को था।

ACTIVITY 9.4

Translate these sentences into English, paying particular attention to the form of the pronouns with postpositions.

1. उस का नाम कविता है।

2. उस लड़की का नाम कविता है।

3. इसका दाम दो रुपये है।

4. जलेबी का दाम दो रुपये है।

5. यह उसका नया मकान है।

6. इस नये मकान का दाम बहुत है।

7. उस बड़े भाई का नाम दीपक है।

8. उसके बड़े भाई का नाम दीपक है।

9. इस अच्छे दोस्त की किताब वहाँ है।

10. उसके अच्छे दोस्त की किताब मेज़ पर है।

11. उस जलेबी की दुकान में जलेबी है।

12. उसकी जलेबी की दुकान में जलेबियाँ हैं।

13. उस छोटे कमरे के पास एक लड़की है।

14. उसके छोटे कमरे के पास एक लड़की है।

ACTIVITY 9.5

Conversation बातचीत

🎧 Read and translate this conversation into English and then listen to it on the online audio. Here Kavita comes to Deepak's uncle's house and meets his sister from Allahabad.

स्थान : दीपक के मामा का घर, नई दिल्ली
पात्र : कविता, दीपक की बहन वृंदा, दीपक

कविता - नमस्कार। मैं दीपक की दोस्त कविता हूँ। तुम्हारा नाम क्या है?
वृन्दा - मेरा नाम वृंदा है। मैं दीपक की बहन हूँ।
कविता - अच्छा, क्या दीपक घर पर है?
वृन्दा - हाँ, अंदर आओ। बैठो। क्या करती हो तुम?
कविता - मैं कॉलेज में पढ़ती हूँ, दीपक के साथ। और तुम?
वृन्दा - मैं भी पढ़ती हूँ, लेकिन इलाहाबाद में। तुम्हारे कितने भाई-बहन हैं?
कविता - मेरा एक भाई है। आजकल वह ऑस्ट्रेलिया में रहता है।
वृन्दा - वे क्या काम करते हैं?
कविता - वह काम नहीं करता। वह भी पढ़ता है।
वृन्दा - तुम क्या पढ़ती हो, डाक्टरी?
कविता - हाँ, मेरा डॉक्टर बनने का इरादा है।*
वृन्दा - अच्छा, मैं दीपक को बुलाती हूँ। अरे हीरालाल! कविता के लिए चाय बनाओ।
कविता - नहीं वृंदा, अभी मुझे चाय नहीं चाहिए। बस पानी पिलाओ।
दीपक - अरे कविता, आजकल तुम मेरे घर क्यों नहीं आतीं?
कविता - दीपक, तुम बहुत बकवास करते हो। मैं अक्सर आती हूँ।
दीपक - अच्छा वृन्दा, तुम कविता को कुछ चाय पिलाओ।
वृन्दा - चाय अभी लाती हूँ, तब तक तुम दोनों बात करो।

* Here the verb बनना *to be made* has the sense of *to become*.

_____

_____

_____

_____

_____

_____

_____

_____

_____

_____

_____

Translate the following questions based on the conversation and then take turns with a partner to ask and answer them. Listen to the online audio and answer these questions in Hindi in the pauses provided.

1. What is Deepak's sister's name? _____

2. Is Deepak at home? _____

3. What does Kavita do? _____

4. Do you study in college? _____

5. Do you work? _____

6. How many brothers and sisters does Kavita have? _____

7. How many brothers and sisters do you have? _____

8. Where does Kavita's brother live? _____

9. Where do you live? _____

10. Does Kavita come to Deepak's house often? _____

Glossary शब्दावली

The following words have appeared in the Activities that accompany Lesson 9. Most are common everyday words. Take a moment to study them along with the genders of the nouns.

अक्सर often
आना to come (*v.i.*)
इतवार Sunday (*m*)
इरादा intention (*m*)
उठना to rise, to get up (*v.i.*)
कब when
कभी-कभी sometimes
करना to do (*v.t.*)
कहना to say (*v.t.*)
काम करना to work (*v.t.*)
के साथ with
गाड़ी car, vehicle, train (*f*)
गुरुवार Thursday (*m*)
जन्मदिन birthday (*m*)
जलेबी jalebi (*f*)

जानना to know (*v.t.*)
जाना to go (*v.i.*)
डॉक्टरी (the practice of) medicine (*f*)
तब तक until then
तोड़ना to break (*v.t.*)
दुकानदार shopkeeper (*m*)
देखना to watch, to see (*v.t.*)
दोनों both
पढ़ना to read, study (*v.t.*)
पत्र letter (*m*)
पहनाना to cause to wear, to dress (*v.t.*)
पहुँचना to arrive (*v.i.*)
पिलाना to cause to drink, to serve (*v.t.*)
पीना to drink (*v.t.*)
फ़िल्म film (*f*)

बकवास nonsense (*f*)
बात करना to talk, converse (*v.t.*)
बैठना to sit (*v.i.*)
मेहनत hard work (*f*)
रहना to live (*v.i.*)
लिखना to write (*v.t.*)
विश्वविद्यालय university (*m*)
शराब alcohol, wine (*f*)
सिखाना to teach (*v.t.*)
सोचना to think (*v.t.*)
सोना to sleep (*v.i.*)
हमेशा always
हर all, every
हीरालाल a name (*m*)

LESSON **10** दसवाँ पाठ

Where Did You Use to Live?

🎧 Complete sentences 1 through 12 with the appropriate form of हूँ, है, हैं, हो or होता है, etc. Then translate them into English. For 13 through 20, translate the sentences into Hindi, remembering to use the correct form of होता है where it is required. Then listen to the sentences on the online audio, repeating them in the pauses provided.

1. हिन्दुस्तानी लड़के सुन्दर .... ।

   ....

2. छै और छै कितने .... ?

   ....

3. आज बहुत गर्मी .... ।

   ....

4. सिगरेट के धुएँ से खाँसी .... ।

   ....

5. भारत में बाघ (pl) .... ।

   ....

6. अमरीका में किताबें महँगी .... ।

   ....

7. भारत में मई के महीने में बहुत गर्मी .... ।

   ....

8. इंदिरा के बस्ते में एक कलम .... ।

   ....

9. इन नेताओं का भरोसा नहीं _____ ।

10. अधिक वर्षा से फ़सल ख़राब _____ ।

11. वह हिन्दुस्तानी लड़की ख़ूबसूरत _____ ।

12. इस नदी का पानी साफ़ नहीं _____ ।

13. Generally Indian people are very generous. _____

14. Hindi is an (one) Indian language. _____

15. The festival of Deepavali takes place in November. (*Deepavali's festival*) _____

16. The sacred Ganges' water is clean. _____

17. On Monday the Hindi('s) class takes place. _____

18. Every Tuesday we have a holiday. (*our holiday is*) _____

19. Muharram is a Muslim festival. (*Muslims' festival*) _____

20. Are the farmers in India very poor? (*India's farmers*) _____

ACTIVITY 10.2

Transform the following sentences from the imperfect present tense to the habitual past and then listen to them on the online audio and repeat them in the pauses provided.

1. सोमवार को मैं कॉलेज जाता हूँ।

2. उस लड़की के पिता जी हर साल हिन्दुस्तान जाते हैं।

3. आप किस जगह वकालत करती हैं?

4. वह सुबह छह बजे उठता है।

_____

5. जनवरी के महीने में माघ का मेला होता है।

_____

6. इतवार को कोई अधिकारी बैंक में नहीं होता।

_____

7. वे लड़कियाँ हिन्दी के अलावा और कुछ नहीं पढ़तीं।

_____

8. मैं अपने माँ-बाप से हिन्दी में ही बोलती हूँ।

_____

9. क्या तुम हर साल अपनी बहन के साथ भारत यात्रा करते हो?

_____

10. शाम को दुकानें बंद रहती हैं।

_____

ACTIVITY 10.3

Translate the following sentences using either अपना or another appropriate pronoun with the postposition का where necessary. Then listen to them on the online audio and repeat them in the pauses provided.

1. Deepak, please give me your book. (Use the imperative form for तुम) _____

2. Put your picture in his house. (Use the imperative form for आप) (to put = to attach) _____

3. Every day she visits her mother. (to visit x = to go near x) _____

4. Please write my name on the paper. (Use the imperative form for आप) _____

5. Don't hand in your work late. (Use the imperative form for तुम) (to hand in = देना to give) _____

🎧 Translate the following sentences into English. Then listen to them on the online audio, repeating them in the pauses provided.

6. रोज़ अपनी हिन्दी की पढ़ाई कीजिए। _____

7. वह आदमी अपने जीवन की कथा सुनाता था। _____

8. क्या आप और आपके पिता जी इलाहाबाद के माघ मेले में जाते थे? _____

_____

9. वह लड़की अपने मन की है। _____

10. अभी अपने कमरे में जा! _____

ACTIVITY 10.4

Conversation बातचीत

🎧 Read and translate this conversation into English and then listen to it on the online audio. Here Kavita and Deepak talk about where they used to live.

स्थान : दीपक के मामा का घर, नई दिल्ली
पात्र : कविता, दीपक

दीपक – कविता, क्या पिछले साल तुम अपने भाई के साथ रहती थीं?

कविता – नहीं जी, लेकिन तीन साल पहले हम दोनों बंबई में रहते थे। मेरे भाई वहाँ पढ़ते थे। क्या पिछले साल तुम दिल्ली में रहते थे?

दीपक – नहीं, हम लोग इलाहाबाद में रहते थे। हमारा घर इलाहाबाद में है।

कविता – अच्छा, तुम्हारी बहन की उम्र क्या है?

दीपक – उसकी उम्र सत्रह साल की है। तुम्हारी उम्र क्या है, कविता?

कविता – मैं बाईस साल की हूँ। और तुम कितने साल के हो?

दीपक – मैं भी बाईस साल का हूँ।

कविता – अच्छा, इलाहाबाद में हर साल माघ मेला होता है, न?

दीपक – हाँ, गंगा और यमुना नदियों में बहुत लोग नहाते हैं।

कविता – वहाँ गंगा, यमुना और सरस्वती, इन तीनों नदियों का संगम होता है, न?

दीपक – हाँ। लेकिन, सरस्वती ज़मीन के नीचे बहती है। ऐसा लोग कहते हैं।

कविता – क्या तुम अपनी बहन के साथ नदी में नहाते थे?

दीपक – बचपन में हमारी माँ हमको नदी में नहलाती थी। माघ मेले में बहुत अच्छा माहौल होता है।

कविता – माघ एक महीने का नाम है, न?

दीपक – हाँ, माघ का महीना जनवरी में पड़ता है।

(lined space for writing)

Translate the following questions based on the conversation and then take turns with a partner to ask and answer them. Listen to the online audio and answer these questions in Hindi in the pauses provided.

1. Did Kavita live with her brother three years ago? _____

2. Did you live with your brother three years ago? _____

3. Where did Kavita live three years ago? _____

4. Where did you live three years ago? _____

5. How old is Kavita? (*of how many years is Kavita?*) _____

6. How old are you? (for numbers, see Textbook p. 151) _____

7. Did Deepak use to bathe in the river in (his) childhood? _____

8. How many rivers meet in Allahabad? _____

Glossary शब्दावली

The following words have appeared in the Activities that accompany Lesson 10. Most are common everyday words. Take a moment to study them along with the genders of the nouns.

अधिक more, too much
अधिकारी official, officer (*m*)
अपना one's own
अपने मन का independent
आम तौर पर generally
इंदिरा a name (*f*)
इक्कीस twenty-one
इसलिये therefore
उदार generous
उम्र age (*f*)
एक साथ together
कक्षा class (*f*)
कथा story (*f*)
कागज़ paper (*m*)
किसान farmer (*m*)
के अलावा in addition to, besides
के नीचे beneath
खाँसी cough (*f*)
गंगा Ganges (*f*)
ग़रीब poor
गर्मी heat (*f*)
छह बजे at six o'clock
जगह place (*f*)
जनवरी January (*f*)
ज़मीन land (*f*)
जीवन life (*m*)
तस्वीर picture (*f*)

तीन साल पहले three years ago
त्यौहार festival (*m*)
दफ़्तर office (*m*)
दिखना to be visible (*v.i.*)
दीपावली Deepavali (*f*)
देर से late (with lateness)
धुआँ smoke (*m*)
नदी river (*f*)
नवम्बर November (*m*)
नहलाना to bathe (someone) (*v.t.*)
नहाना to bathe (*v.t.* + *v.i.*)
नाच dance (*m*)
नाटक drama (*m*)
नेता leader, politician (*m*)*
पड़ना to fall (*v.i.*)
पवित्र sacred
पहले ago, previously
बंद रहना to remain closed (*v.i.*)
बंबई Bombay (*f*)
बचपन childhood (*m*)
बस्ता (school) bag (*m*)
बहना to flow (*v.i.*)
बाईस twenty-two
बाघ tiger (*m*)
बीस twenty
बोलना to speak (*v.t.* + *v.i.*)
भरोसा faith, trust (*m*)

भारत India (*m*)
मई May (*f*)
महँगा expensive
माघ the name of a month (*m*)
माहौल atmosphere (*m*)
मिलना to meet (*v.i.*)
मुसलमान Muslim (*m*)
मुहर्रम the month of Imam Hussain's
  martyrdom which is held sacred
  and celebrated by Shia Muslims
मेला fair (*m*)
यमुना Yamuna (*f*)
यात्रा करना to travel (*v.t.*)
लगाना to attach (*v.t.*)
वकालत advocacy (*f*)
वर्ष year (*m*)
वर्षा rain (*f*)
संगम confluence (*m*)
सत्रह seventeen
सरस्वती Sarasvati (*f*)
साफ़ clear, clean
साल year (*m*)
सिगरेट cigarette (*f*)
सुनाना to tell, relate (*v.t.*)
सुबह morning (*f*)
हिन्दुस्तानी Indian

* This declines like राजा (see Textbook p. 54).

LESSON 11 ग्यारहवाँ पाठ

What Do You Study?

Translate these sentences. Then listen to them on the online audio and repeat them in the pauses provided.

1. उस कमरे में बैठो और अपना काम करो। ⸺⸺⸺⸺⸺⸺⸺⸺⸺⸺

2. वह और उस की माँ छुट्टियों में लखनऊ जाते थे। ⸺⸺⸺⸺⸺⸺

3. अपने बस्ते से मेरी कॉपी निकालो। ⸺⸺⸺⸺⸺⸺⸺⸺⸺⸺

4. तुम अपने-आप अपना हिन्दी का काम करती हो, न? ⸺⸺⸺⸺⸺

5. वे ख़ुद वहाँ क्यों नहीं जाते थे? ⸺⸺⸺⸺⸺⸺⸺⸺⸺⸺

6. I do all my (own) work myself. (ख़ुद) ⸺⸺⸺⸺⸺⸺⸺⸺

7. Look at yourself in the mirror. (अपने-आप)* ⸺⸺⸺⸺⸺⸺
   * Remember that the objects of these verbs (देखना, कहना) are animate and denote a particular being.

8. Rajaneesh used to call himself Lord. (अपने-आप)* ⸺⸺⸺⸺
   * See the note above.

9. Why do you talk to yourself? (अपने-आप)* ⸺⸺⸺⸺⸺⸺⸺
   * In Hindi when we talk to someone, we talk or speak *with* them. Therefore, in place of को the object of this sentence will have to take से *with*. There are four or five such verbs that involve speaking, talking, asking, conversing, etc., that follow the same pattern (see Textbook, p. 154).

10. The world changes (by) itself. (अपने-आप) ⸺⸺⸺⸺⸺⸺⸺

11. This door is automatic (*opens by itself*). (अपने-आप) ⸺⸺⸺⸺

ACTIVITY 11.2

 Read this passage and listen to it on the online audio. Then answer the questions below in Hindi.

एक बार एक लड़का दिल्ली में रहता था। उस का नाम दीपक था। अक्सर वह बाज़ार जाता और वहाँ से अपनी एक ख़ास दोस्त कविता के घर जाता। अगर उसकी दोस्त इतनी दूर न रहती तो शायद दीपक रोज़ उस के घर जाता। हफ़्ते में दो बार वे दोनों अपने दोस्तों के घर में भी मिलते थे। उस की दोस्त भी कभी-कभी उस के पास आती। दोनों बहुत देर तक देश और समाज के बारे में खूब बातचीत करते। वह लड़की कहती थी कि अगर भारत की आबादी इतनी नहीं होती तो लोगों की ज़िन्दगी और अच्छी होती। अक्सर वह सरकार को भी पत्र लिखती। लेकिन सरकार इस के बारे में किसी की बात सुनती तो शायद इतनी समस्याएँ नहीं होतीं।

1. लड़के का नाम क्या था? ....

2. वह कहाँ रहता था? ....

3. लड़का कविता के घर कब जाता था? ....

4. अगर कविता इतनी दूर न रहती तो लड़का क्या करता? ....

5. दोनों किस के बारे में बातचीत करते थे? ....

ACTIVITY 11.3

 Translate these sentences into Hindi following the example, and then listen to them on the online audio and repeat them in the pauses provided. All of the statements are contrary to fact. Words in italics indicate that the verb is to be placed in the form that indicates that the statement is contrary to fact.

If you (*m*) *had gone* to university that day then I (*m*) *would have met* you.
अगर उस दिन आप विश्वविद्यालय जाते तो मैं आप से मिलता।

1. If he *had watched* television last night then he *would have seen* a Hindi film.

   ....

2. If his mother *had come* this morning then he *would have taken* her to the market. (x को ले जाना to take x)

   ....

3. If Deepak *had given* Kavita flowers that night then they *would have become* friends. (*their friendship would have happened*) (होना to become, happen)

   ....

4. If the rent of this house *weren't* so much then *I would live* here.

   ....

ACTIVITY 11.4

Write answers to these questions paying particular attention to the adverbs of time that have been used in them. Then listen to the online audio and repeat your answers in the pauses provided.

1. रोज़ सुबह तुम कितने बजे उठते हो? (उठती हो) _____

2. पिछले साल तुम कहाँ रहते थे? (रहती थीं) _____

3. हफ़्ते में रात को तुम कितने बजे सोते हो? (सोती हो) _____

4. वीक-एंड में रात को तुम कितने बजे सोते हो? (सोती हो) _____

5. क्या तुम हर हफ़्ते सोमवार की सुबह शहर जाते हो? (जाती हो) _____

6. तुम मंगल की सुबह कितने बजे नाश्ता करते हो? (करती हो) _____

7. रोज़ शाम को क्या तुम चाय पीते हो? (पीती हो) _____

ACTIVITY 11.5

Conversation बातचीत

Read and translate this conversation into English and then listen to it on the online audio. Here Kavita and Deepak go shopping for a online audio by Abida Parveen.

स्थान : संगीत की दुकान, नई दिल्ली
पात्र : कविता, दीपक

दीपक - कविता, तुम्हें किस की सी॰ डी॰ चाहिये?
कविता - मुझे आबिदा परवीन[1] की एक सी॰ डी॰ चाहिये। मैं उनका संगीत बहुत सुनती हूँ।
दीपक - चलो, हम इस दुकान में देखते हैं।
कविता - ठीक है। यह दुकान बहुत पुरानी है। मेरे माँ-बाप इस दुकान से संगीत का सामान ख़रीदते थे।
दीपक - आबिदा परवीन का संगीत कैसा होता है?
कविता - तुम नहीं जानते?
दीपक - अगर मैं उन के बारे में जानता तो क्या मैं यह सवाल पूछता?
कविता - तो उनकी एक सी॰ डी॰ लो न, और सुनो। वे पूरी दुनिया में बहुत मशहूर हैं।
दीपक - क्या वे क़व्वाली गाती हैं?
कविता - हाँ, क़व्वाली और ग़ज़ल गाती हैं। वे अक्सर हिन्दुस्तान आती हैं। पिछले साल अगर हमारी जान-पहचान होती तो मैं तुमको उनके कॉनसर्ट में ले जाती।
दीपक - वह बहुत अच्छा होता। कविता, क्या इस दुकान में मोलतोल होता है?
कविता - दीपक, यह ऐसी दुकान नहीं है।
दीपक - यहाँ अगर मोलतोल होता तो मैं बहुत चीज़ें ख़रीदता।
कविता - दीपक! तुम बहुत ज़्यादा कंजूस हो! क्या तुम्हें कोई सी॰ डी॰ नहीं चाहिये?
दीपक - ठीक है, मैं नुसरत फ़तह अली ख़ान[2] की एक सी॰ डी॰ लेता हूँ।

---

1. A famous Sufi singer from Pakistan.
2. A famous qawali singer from Pakistan.

Translate the following questions based on the conversation and then take turns with a partner to ask and answer them. Listen to the online audio and answer these questions in Hindi in the pauses provided.

1. To whose music does Kavita listen? _____

_____

2. Is the music shop very old? _____

_____

3. If Deepak knew about Abida Parveen then would he have asked? _____

_____

4. Do you listen to Abida Parveen's music? _____

_____

5. Does bargaining take place in this shop? _____

_____

6. If there were bargaining in the shop, would Deepak buy many things? _____

_____

7. Whose CD does Deepak buy? _____

_____

Glossary शब्दावली

The following words have appeared in the Activities that accompany Lesson 11. Most are common everyday words. Take a moment to study them along with the genders of the nouns.

अगर if (*conj*)

अपने-आप (by) oneself

आइना mirror (*m*)

आबादी population (*f*)

इस तरह in this way

कंजूस miserly, miser

क़रीब near

क़व्वाली qawali (a genre of devotional song) (*f*)

कहना to say, to call (x something) (*v.t.*)

कॉनसर्ट concert (*m*)

की तरह like

के पास near

के बारे में about

ख़ास special

ख़ुद (by) oneself

खुलना to open (*v.i.*)

ख़ूब a lot, excellent

ग़ज़ल a genre of Urdu poetry that is also sung (*f*)

गाना to sing (*v.t.*)

चीज़ thing (*f*)

छोड़ना to leave, abandon (*v.t.*)

ज़माना age, period (*m*)

ज़िन्दगी life (*f*)

टेलीविज़न television (*m*)

ठीक से properly

दरवाज़ा door (*m*)

दूर far

देर delay, late (*f*)

देश country (*m*)

दोस्ती friendship (*f*)

निकालना to take out (*v.t.*)

पूछना to ask (*v.t.*)

बदलना to change (*v.t. + v.i.*)

बनना to be made, to become (*v.i.*)

बहुत देर तक for a long time

बातचीत करना to converse (x से) (*v.t.*)

बार time, turn (*f*)

बुरा bad

भई brother, friend (*m*)

भगवान Lord (God) (*m*)

मज़ाक joke (*m*)

मशहूर famous

x को मानना to accept x (*v.t.*)

मोलतोल haggling, bargaining (*m*)

रजनीश name (*m*)

लखनऊ Lucknow (*m*)

ले जाना to take (away) (*v.i.*)

लेना to take, buy (*v.t.*)

विचार thought (*m*)

शायद perhaps

संगीत music (*m*)

समझना to regard, consider, understand (*v.i.*)

समस्या problem (*f*)

समाज society (*m*)

सरकार government (*f*)

सवाल question (*m*)

सवेरा morning (*m*)

सी॰ डी॰ CD (*f*)

सुनना to hear, listen (*v.t.*)

हफ़्ता week (*m*)

LESSON 12 बारहवाँ पाठ

Where Were You Born?
Where Did You Grow Up?

ACTIVITY 12.1

Transform the sentences from the imperfect present tense to the past tense following the example. Then translate them into English.

क्या तुम हिन्दुस्तान जाते हो?
Do you go to India?

क्या तुम हिन्दुस्तान गये?
Did you go to India?

1. वह रात को दस बजे सोती है।

2. हम दिल्ली में रहते हैं।

3. आप सोमवार को कहाँ जाती हैं?

4. मैं अपना खाना लाती हूँ।

5. यह ठीक समय पर क्यों नहीं उठता?

6. गुरुवार को एक आदमी आता है।

7. सभी भाषाएँ क्यों बदलती हैं?

8. तुम कॉलेज कितने बजे पहुँचते हो?

9. क्या आपकी बातें उससे होती हैं?

10. दुकानें नौ बजे खुलती हैं।

ACTIVITY 12.2

Translate the following sentences into Hindi and then listen to them on the online audio and repeat them in the pauses provided.

1. He went (*in*) to the shop and he bought some vegetables.

2. We read one of Premchand's stories in class. (*Premchand's one story*)

3. Yesterday I saw a good film with my friend.

4. What happened last week in class?

5. She brought her (*own*) friend into the class.

6. My brother got up at six o'clock this morning.

7. He met his (*own*) sisters' friend in university that day. (*met with ... on that day*)

8. I will return right now. (*I've right now come*)

9. Who saw the film called *Om Shanti Om*? (*who saw* ॐ शान्ति ॐ *called film?*)

10. Last night what did you do?

ACTIVITY 12.3

Conversation बातचीत

Read and translate this conversation into English and then listen to it on the online audio. Here Kavita meets Deepak after she has returned from a trip to Lucknow.

स्थान : दीपक के मामा का घर, नई दिल्ली
पात्र : कविता, दीपक

कविता - नमस्ते दीपक, तुम्हारा मिज़ाज कैसा है?

दीपक - अरे कविता, अंदर आओ। तुम इतने दिनों से कहाँ थीं?

कविता - मैं लखनऊ में थी। क्या तुम कभी लखनऊ गये?

दीपक - मैं कभी नहीं गया। तुम लखनऊ क्यों गयीं?

कविता - अक्सर पिता जी का कुछ न कुछ काम लखनऊ में होता है। तो वे कभी-कभी वहाँ जाते हैं। इस बार मैं भी उनके साथ गयी।

दीपक - तो तुमने लखनऊ में क्या-क्या किया?

कविता - मैंने बस आराम किया। सवेरे बहुत देर तक सोती थी। हमारे कुछ रिश्तेदार लखनऊ में रहते हैं। हम उनके साथ रहे। उनके साथ मैं बड़ा इमामबाड़ा देखने के लिये भी गयी।

दीपक - बड़ा इमामबाड़ा क्या चीज़ होती है?

कविता - वह एक बहुत खूबसूरत इमारत है। किसी नवाब ने उसे बनवाया।

दीपक - क्या तुम उस नवाब का नाम नहीं जानतीं?

कविता - हाँ, जानती हूँ। उन का नाम आसफुद्दौला था। अठारहवीं शताब्दी में उन्होंने बड़ा इमामबाड़ा बनवाया। वे बहुत दानी नवाब थे।

दीपक - वाह, तुमने लखनऊ के बारे में काफ़ी सीखा। अच्छा, लखनऊ में तुमने क्या-क्या और किया?

कविता - बहुत कुछ नहीं। इस बीच ईद का त्यौहार था। तो हम अपने रिश्तेदारों के कुछ दोस्तों के घर गये।

दीपक - तो ईद के दिन लोग क्या करते हैं?

कविता - अगर अभी वक़्त होता तो मैं तुम्हें बताती।

_____

_____

_____

_____

_____

_____

_____

_____

_____

🎧 Translate the following questions based on the conversation and then take turns with a partner to ask and answer them. Listen to the online audio and answer these questions in Hindi in the pauses provided.

1. Where was Kavita last week? _____

_____

2. Has Deepak ever been (gone) to Lucknow? _____

_____

3. Have you been to Lucknow? _____

_____

4. Have you been to India? _____

_____

5. Does Kavita's father go to Lucknow occasionally (sometimes)? _____

_____

6. Did Kavita stay with her relatives in Lucknow? _____

_____

7. Do you stay with your (own) relatives in India? _____

_____

8. Did Kavita go with relatives to their friends' home? _____

_____

Glossary शब्दावली

The following words have appeared in the Activities that accompany Lesson 12. Most are common everyday words. Take a moment to study them along with the genders of the nouns.

अट्ठारहवाँ eighteenth

आराम करना to relax (*v.t.*)

आसफ़ुद्दौला Asaf-ud-Daula (one of the most famous Nawabs of the independent Kingdom of Oudh, the capital of which was Lucknow)

इमारत building (*f*)

इस बीच meanwhile, in the meantime

ईद Eid (a Muslim festival at the end of Ramadan to celebrate the end of fasting) (*f*)

कभी ever, sometime

कल रात last night

कितने बजे at what time?

x की बात y से होना for x's conversation to take place with y (*v.i.*)

कुछ और some (thing) more

कुछ-न-कुछ something or other

क्या-क्या what (the reduplication gives a sense of plural)

ख़रीदना to buy (*v.t.*)

छै बजे six o'clock

जमात class (*f*)

दस बजे ten o'clock

दानी generous

नवाब Nawab (a Muslim noble or ruler) (*m*)

नामक called

प्रेमचंद name of a famous Hindi author (*m*)

बड़ा इमामबाड़ा Bara Imambara (one of the famous historical buildings in Lucknow) (*m*)

बनवाना to cause to be built (*v.t.*)

बस enough, just

मिज़ाज mood, temperament (*m*)

रिश्तेदार relative (*m*)

वाला the one which

शताब्दी century (*f*)

सब्ज़ी vegetable (*f*)

से from, since

LESSON **13** तेरहवाँ पाठ

Do You Have Money?

ACTIVITY 13.1

🎧 Complete the following sentences using the appropriate postposition. Then translate them into English. Listen to them on the online audio and repeat them in the spaces provided.

1. क्या इस साल आप .... गाड़ी है?

   ....

2. अभी उस .... कितने पैसे हैं?

   ....

3. मेरी माँ .... दो बहनें हैं।

   ....

4. हमारे घर .... दो कमरे हैं।

   ....

5. उस मामले में इस .... क्या विचार थे?

   ....

6. अभी मेरी मदद करने के लिये क्या शिक्षक .... समय है?

   ....

7. बताइये, आप .... कितने सवाल हैं?

   ....

8. भारतीय महिला .... क्या-क्या विशेष गुण होते हैं?

   ....

9. उन .... किताबें पढ़ने का शौक़ है।

   ....

10. क्या आप _____ हिम्मत है?

11. वह एक बहुत बड़े पेड़ _____ खड़ा था।

12. सीधे डॉक्टर _____ इलाज के लिये जाओ।

13. घड़ी _____ दो सुइयाँ होती थीं।

14. कक्षा में आप _____ कौन बैठता है?

15. क्या दीपक _____ कुछ ज़मीन थी?

ACTIVITY 13.2

Translate the sentences following the example, and then listen to them on the online audio. Repeat them in the pauses provided.

Do you have shoes to play tennis?   क्या टेनिस खेलने के लिये आपके पास जूते हैं?

1. Do you have money to eat? (*for eating food*)

2. Did he have the time to go swimming? (*did he have the time for swimming*)

3. Did you give her a tablet to get rid of her headache? (*for getting rid of*)

4. Did you give them the money to go to India? (*for going*)

5. She doesn't have a (*any*) book to read. (*for reading*)

6. At the end of the year, please come to India to study Hindi. (*for studying Hindi*)

   ....

7. It is better to learn Hindi in India. (*in India learning Hindi more good is*)

   ....

8. Come to the city to see a film. (*for seeing film city come*) ....

   ....

9. We went to the market to buy some goods. (*for taking*; use लेना *to take*) ....

   ....

ACTIVITY 13.3

🎧 Complete the sentences in the present perfect tense following the example. Then translate them and listen to them on the online audio, repeating them in the pauses provided.

मैं (*m*) अभी आप से मिलने को आया हूँ ‌‌ । (आना *to come*)
I (*m*) have come to meet you right now.

1. क्या आपने ये किताबें .... ? (ख़रीदना *to buy*)

   ....

2. तुम (*m*) मेरी कुर्सी पर क्यों .... ? (बैठना *to sit*)

   ....

3. उस की शादी किसी भारतीय महिला से .... । (होना *to occur*)

   ....

4. हम (*f*) दोबारा भारत .... । (आना *to come*)

   ....

5. उन्होंने अभी-अभी अपना काम पूरा .... । (करना *to do*)

   ....

6. वह (*m*) भारत से अमरीका दो हफ़्ते के लिये .... । (आना *to come*)

   ....

Now transform them all into the past perfect following the example. Then translate them and listen to them on the online audio, repeating them in the pauses provided.

कल मैं *(f)* आप से मिलने आयी थी।   (आना to come)
Yesterday I came to meet you.

7. क्या आपने ये किताबें _____ ? (ख़रीदना to buy)

_____

8. तुम *(m)* मेरी कुर्सी पर क्यों _____ ? (बैठना to sit)

_____

9. उस की शादी किसी भारतीय महिला से _____ । (होना to occur)

_____

10. हम *(f)* दोबारा भारत _____ । (आना to come)

_____

11. उन्होंने अभी-अभी अपना काम पूरा _____ । (करना to do)

_____

12. वह *(m)* भारत से अमरीका दो हफ़्ते के लिये _____ । (आना to come)

_____

ACTIVITY 13.4

Conversation बातचीत

Read and translate this conversation into English and then listen to it on the online audio. Here Deepak and Kavita discuss going to have dinner at the Bengali Market.

स्थान : दिल्ली विश्वविद्यालय, नई दिल्ली
पात्र : कविता, दीपक

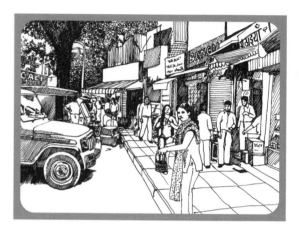

दीपक – कविता, क्या तुम आज पुरानी दिल्ली खाने को जाना चाहती हो?

कविता – आज नहीं। बंगाली मार्केट क्यों नहीं चलते? मैं बहुत दिनों से वहाँ नहीं गयी।

दीपक – मैं दो दिन पहले वहाँ गया था। लेकिन ठीक है, हम वहाँ चलते हैं। वहाँ की चाट बहुत अच्छी होती है।

कविता – हाँ, और पिछले हफ़्ते मैंने अख़बार में पढ़ा था कि चाट की एक नयी दुकान वहाँ खुली है। मैंने सुना है कि वहाँ की आलू की टिकिया बहुत खाने लायक़ है। लोग कहते हैं कि नयी दुकान का खाना बहुत चटपटा और मज़ेदार होता है।

दीपक – वह तो ठीक है। पर मैं बंगाली स्वीट हाउस* में खाना चाहता हूँ।

कविता – वहाँ मैंने बहुत बार खाया है। किसी नयी जगह क्यों नहीं चलते?

दीपक – ठीक है। तुम्हारे पास कितना वक़्त है?

कविता – मेरे पास लगभग एक घंटा है। मैं अभी माँ को फ़ोन करती हूँ, बताने के लिये कि क्या प्रोग्राम है।

दीपक – ठीक है। क्या आज तुम्हारे पास गाड़ी है?

कविता – नहीं, आज मैं मेट्रो से आयी हूँ।

दीपक – अच्छा, कोई बात नहीं। मेरे पास गाड़ी है। चलो, अभी चलते हैं।

* A well-known restaurant in Bengali Market, New Delhi.

Translate the following questions based on the conversation and then take turns with a partner to ask and answer them. Listen to the online audio and answer these questions in Hindi in the pauses provided.

1. Where does Deepak want to go to eat today? _____

2. Do you want to go out to eat tonight? _____

3. Does Kavita want to go to Old Delhi to eat? _____

4. How many days ago did Deepak go to the Bengali Market? _____

5. Is the *chat* in the Bengali Market (generally) very good? _____

6. What had Kavita read in the newspaper last week? _____

7. What do people say about the new store in Bengali Market? _____

8. How much time does Kavita have? _____

9. Has Kavita come to university by the metro today? _____

10. Does Deepak have a car today? _____

Glossary शब्दावली

The following words have appeared in the Activities that accompany Lesson 13. Most are common everyday words. Take a moment to study them along with the genders of the nouns.

अंत end (*m*)	ज़्यादा more	लायक़ worthy, capable, able
अभी-अभी right now	टिकिया a small cake, tablet, patty (*f*)	वक़्त time (*m*)
आलू potato (*m*)	दूर करना to dispel, get rid of (*v.t.*)	शहर city (*m*)
इलाज remedy, treatment (*m*)	दोबारा twice, a second time	शादी wedding, marriage (*f*)
कुर्सी/कुरसी chair (*f*)	पिछले हफ़्ते last week	शिक्षक teacher (*m*)
कोई बात नहीं no matter	पुराना old	शौक़ interest, hobby (*m*)
गुण quality (*m*)	पूरा करना to complete (*v.t.*)	साल year (*m*)
गोली tablet, pill, bullet (*f*)	मज़ेदार tasty, enjoyable	सिरदर्द headache (*m*)
घंटा hour (*m*)	x की मदद करना to help x (*v.t.*)	सीधे straight (direction)
चटपटा pungent, spicy	महिला woman (*f*)	सुई needle, hand of a watch (*f*)
चलना to move, go (*v.i.*)	मामला issue (*m*)	सुनना to hear (*v.t.*)
जवाब देना to answer (*v.t.*)	लगभग approximately	हिम्मत courage (*f*)

LESSON 14 चौदहवाँ पाठ

How Long Have You Been Learning Hindi?

ACTIVITY 14.1

🎧 Complete the sentences following the example, and then translate them. Listen to the online audio and repeat them in the pauses provided.

मैं (f) अभी अपनी पढ़ाई कर रही हूँ। (करना to do)

I (f) am doing my study right now.

1. मैं (m) अभी घर _____। (जाना to go)

   _____

2. हम (m) अभी एक दोस्त के घर में हिन्दी _____। (सीखना to learn)

   _____

3. तो तू (f) अभी क्या _____? (करना to do)

   _____

4. तुम (m) यही किताब क्यों _____? (पढ़ना to study, read)

   _____

5. आप (f) अभी किस को चिट्ठी _____? (लिखना to write)

   _____

6. आज भी बहुत ठंड (f) _____। (होना to be, occur)

   _____

7. वह लड़का तो कमरे में दूध _____। (पीना to drink)

   _____

8. सभी लड़कियाँ ऊपर तो नहीं _____। (सोना to sleep)

   _____

ACTIVITY 14.2

Complete the sentences following the example, and then translate them. Listen to the online audio and repeat them in the pauses provided.

उस समय वह (m) नहा रहा था।   (नहाना to bathe)

At that time he was bathing.

1. कल ही दिन में मैं (f) यह काम _____। (करना to do)

   _____

2. कल रात को भी वह (m) पुस्तकालय में _____। (पढ़ना to study, read)

   _____

3. उस समय हम (m) बग़ीचे में _____। (टहलना to stroll)

   _____

4. कल दो बजे उससे बातें _____। (होना to be, become, occur)

   _____

5. तभी यह लड़की खिड़की _____। (खोलना to open)

   _____

6. जी, मेरे पिता जी उस समय उस दुकान में कुछ सामान _____। (ख़रीदना to buy)

   _____

7. वहीं कुछ आदमी खाना _____। (खाना to eat)

   _____

ACTIVITY 14.3

Answer the questions substituting भी or ही in your answer, following the example. Then listen to the online audio and repeat your answers in the pauses provided.

क्या तुम्हारे भाई भी हिन्दी पढ़ते हैं?   जी नहीं, मेरे भाई ही हिन्दी पढ़ते हैं।

Do your brothers also study Hindi?   No, only my brothers study Hindi. (no one else)

1. क्या तुम हिन्दुस्तान भी जाते हो?   _____
   (f – जाती हो)   No, I only go to India. (nowhere else)

2. क्या तुम हिन्दी बोलते ही हो?
   (*f* – बोलती हो)

No, I also speak Hindi. (also read/write it, etc.)

3. क्या तुम भी गाड़ी चलाते हो?
   (*f* – चलाती हो)

No, only I drive a car. (no one else)

4. क्या तुम हिन्दी ही पढ़ते हो?
   (*f* – पढ़ती हो)

No, I also study Hindi. (along with other subjects)

5. क्या तुम्हीं हिन्दी लिखते हो?
   (*f* – लिखती हो)

No, I also write Hindi. (along with others)

ACTIVITY 14.4

Translate the following sentences into Hindi and then listen to them on the online audio, repeating them in the pauses provided. Use आप for all second person pronouns.

1. Do you study at (*in*) university? (present imperfect)

2. Yes, I study at (*in*) university.

3. Have you ever been (gone) to university? (present perfect)

4. Yes, I have been to university.

5. Are you going to university right now? (present progressive)

6. No, I am not going to university right now.

7. Did you go to university yesterday? (past)

8. Yes, I went to university yesterday.

9. Were you going to university yesterday at three o'clock? (past progressive)

10. No, I wasn't going to university yesterday at three o'clock.

11. I was going to my (own) mother's home.

12. Had you gone to university last week? (past perfect)

13. No, last week was a holiday.

14. If you had gone to university today then would you have gone to the library? (contrary to fact)

15. Yes, if I had gone to university today then I would have gone to the library.

16. Did you (use to) go to university last year? (habitual past)

17. No, last year I didn't (use to) go to university.

ACTIVITY 14.5

Conversation बातचीत

Read and translate this conversation into English and then listen to it on the online audio. Here Deepak sees Kavita in Khan Market while walking to his car. He is off to the station to pick up his father, who is returning from Allahabad.

स्थान : ख़ान मार्केट, नई दिल्ली
पात्र : कविता, दीपक

दीपक - अरे कविता, तुम अभी यहाँ क्या कर रही हो?
कविता - माँ के साथ मैं कुछ सामान ख़रीदने आयी हूँ। माँ दुकान में गयी हैं। क्यों?
दीपक - मैं अभी पिता जी को लेने के लिये स्टेशन जा रहा हूँ। अपनी गाड़ी से जा रहा हूँ। मेरे साथ चलो।
कविता - अच्छा, तुम्हारे पिता जी आ रहे हैं?
दीपक - हाँ, इलाहाबाद से आ रहे हैं।

कविता - तुमने बताया क्यों नहीं था? अच्छा, मैं भी चलती हूँ। एक मिनट, मैं माँ को बताती हूँ। तुम्हारे पिता जी किस रेलगाड़ी से आ रहे हैं?

दीपक - प्रयाग एक्सप्रेस से। वह तो दोपहर को तीन बजे पहुँचती है।

कविता - तो हमारे पास आधा घंटा ही है। चलो।

दीपक - कल तुम कॉलेज नहीं गयीं? तुम क्या कर रही थीं?

कविता - मैं गयी थी, जी! दोपहर को मैं लाइब्रेरी में चिकित्सा की एक किताब पढ़ रही थी। उस समय तुम क्या कर रहे थे?

दीपक - मैं भी कॉलेज में था। मुझे तुम्हारी एक किताब चाहिये थी।

कविता - अच्छा, तो तुम मुझे ढूँढने के लिये लाइब्रेरी में क्यों नहीं आये?

दीपक - मैं गया था। पर मैंने तुम्हें नहीं देखा। अच्छा देखो, स्टेशन सामने है। तीन नम्बर प्लैटफ़ार्म पर चलो।

कविता - गाड़ी उधर है। सामने देखो।

दीपक - हाँ, हाँ। और वे पिता जी दिखाई दे रहे हैं। वे अपना हाथ हिला रहे हैं। उन्होंने हमें देखा है।

Translate the following questions based on the conversation and then take turns with a partner to ask and answer them. Listen to the online audio and answer these questions in Hindi in the pauses provided.

1. What is Kavita doing right now?

2. What are you doing right now?

3. With whom has Kavita come to the market?

4. Where is Deepak going right now?

5. Why is Deepak going to the station?

6. Who is coming from Allahabad?

7. Had Kavita gone to college yesterday?

8. What had Deepak wanted yesterday?

9. On which platform is the train coming? (which किस)

Glossary शब्दावली

The following words have appeared in the Activities that accompany Lesson 14. Most are common everyday words. Take a moment to study them along with the genders of the nouns.

आधा half

एक्सप्रेस express

खिड़की window (*f*)

घंटा hour, bell (*m*)

चलना to move (*v.i.*)

चाचा paternal uncle (*m*)

चिकित्सा remedy, treatment (*f*)

चिट्ठी letter (*f*)

टहलना to stroll (*v.i.*)

ठंड cold (*f*)

ढूँढना to search (*v.t.*)

तीन बजे at three o'clock

दिखाई देना to be visible (*v.i.*)

दूध milk (*m*)

दो बजे at two o'clock

दोपहर midday, afternoon (*f*)

पिछले हफ़्ते last week

पुस्तकालय library (*m*)

प्रयाग Prayag (Allahabad) (*m*)

प्लैटफ़ार्म platform (*m*)

बग़ीचा garden (*m*)

यही this very (person, thing)

रिश्तेदार relative (*m*)

रेलगाड़ी train (*f*)

स्टेशन station (*m*)

हाथ hand, arm (*m*)

हिलाना to shake, wave (*v.t.*)

LESSON **15** पंद्रहवाँ पाठ

Student Life in Delhi

Translate the following sentences. Remember that they are all contrary to fact statements.

1. अगर वह हमारे साथ रहता तो हम उसे अपने देश के बारे में सिखाते।

_____

2. अगर वह हमारे साथ रहा होता तो हम उसे अपने देश के बारे में सिखाते।

_____

3. अभी बात उस की समझ में आ रही होती तो मैं उस की मदद करती।

_____

4. अगर आप हिन्दुस्तान गये होते तो आप की हिन्दी तो बहुत अच्छी होती।

_____

5. यदि वह विश्वविद्यालय आया होता तो उसने भी यह हिन्दी फ़िल्म देखी होती।

_____

6. अगर आप गंगा नदी में नहातीं तो आप के सब पाप मिटते।

_____

7. तुमने यही सवाल नहीं पूछा होता तो मैं उस बात के बारे में नहीं सोचती।

_____

8. अगर ये इस लेख को पढ़तीं तो गांधी जी के बारे में कुछ जानतीं।

_____

9. यदि तूने क़लम ख़रीदी होती तो इम्तहान में यह दिक़्क़त नहीं होती।

_____

10. अगर आपने मुझे बुलाया होता तो मैं आपके पास आया होता।

_____

11. यदि मेरे पास पैसा होता तो मैं भी गुलाबजामुन खाता।

_____

12. मेरा भाई शरबत पीता तो उसकी प्यास बुझी होती।

_____

13. आप अपना सब काम करते तो आप परीक्षा में पास होते।

_____

14. If I had read this book then I would have given it to you.

_____

15. If you had time then you would have come (in order to) see me in the hospital.

_____

16. If my car hadn't broken (down) then I would have driven it. (use ख़राब होना to break, be spoiled)

_____

17. If Kavita had cooked the food then the family would have eaten.

_____

18. If I hadn't studied Hindi then I would have studied Bengali.

_____

19. If they were studying in the library right now, then I would search for them. (*I would do their search*)

_____

ACTIVITY 15.2

Translate the following questions using कुछ or कोई appropriately. Then answer them according to the direction in parentheses. Listen to the online audio and repeat your answers in the pauses provided.

1. Is *some* woman standing in that room? (yes) _____

   _____

2. Do I (*m*) know *something* about India? (no) _____

   _____

3. Do *some* people study Hindi with you? (yes) _____

   _____

4. Did *no one* else use to study Hindi with you? (yes) _____

   _____

5. Did your friend study *some* Hindi with you last year? (yes) _____

   _____

6. Do the students want to learn *everything* about grammar? (no) _____

   _____

7. Is *anyone else* coming to the city now? (no) _____

   _____

8. Is there *some* tea in your cup? (yes) _____

   _____

9. Does *anyone* need *some* help? (yes) _____

   _____

ACTIVITY 15.3

Combine the sentences using the absolutive कर construction, following the example. Translate them and then listen to them on the online audio, repeating them in the pauses provided.

अपना नाम और पता काग़ज़ पर लिखिये। मुझे दीजिये।
अपना नाम और पता काग़ज़ पर लिखकर मुझे दीजिए।

Please write your name and address on a piece of paper and give it to me.

1. उसने अपना काम किया। वह बाहर गया।

2. हम शहर जाते हैं। हम फ़िल्में देखते हैं।

3. मेरे कमरे में आइये। इस कुर्सी पर बैठिये।

4. तुमने दो किताबें लीं। तुम आये थे।

5. वह छात्रा हिन्दुस्तान गयी। वहाँ उसने हिन्दी सीखी।

6. मेरी माँ ने मेरे कपड़े लिये। वह अपने घर गयी।

7. सभी लोग ध्यान देते थे। सभी लोग शिक्षिका की बात सुनते थे।

8. लोग इलाहाबाद जाते थे। लोग गंगा में नहाते थे।

9. मुझे मेरी किताब दो। जाओ।

10. उस को चिट्ठी लिखना। सभी बातें बताना।

ACTIVITY 15.4

Conversation बातचीत

Read and translate this conversation into English and then listen to it on the online audio. Here Kavita tells Deepak something about the Muslim festival of Eid.

स्थान : कविता का घर, नई दिल्ली

पात्र : कविता, दीपक

दीपक - कविता, तुमने ईद के बारे में मुझे कुछ नहीं बताया।

कविता - ठीक है, बताती हूँ। ईद मुसलमानों के लिये बहुत महत्त्वपूर्ण त्यौहार है। ईद की कहानी बहुत पुरानी भी है। ईद साल में कई बार मनाते हैं।

दीपक - तो बताओ यह कौन-सी ईद है?

कविता - कुछ लोग इसको ईद-उज़-ज़ुहा कहते हैं, तो कुछ लोग इसे ईद-उल-अज़हा कहते हैं। लेकिन आम तौर पर बच्चे इसे बक़रईद कहते हैं। इस त्यौहार में लोग किसी जानवर का बलिदान देकर मस्जिद में नमाज़ पढ़ कर ख़ुदा को याद करते हैं।

दीपक - लखनऊ नवाबी तहज़ीब के लिये बहुत मशहूर है, न?

कविता - हाँ, और ईद के वक़्त वहाँ माहौल बहुत शानदार होता है।

दीपक - अच्छा! मैं लखनऊ गया होता तो मैं भी यह सब देखता।

कविता - अगली बार हमारे साथ आकर लखनऊ देखना।

दीपक - लखनऊ के बारे में कुछ और बताना, कविता।

कविता - अभी अगर मैं अपने घर नहीं जा रही होती तो मैं कई बातें बताती। पर अभी मेरे पास समय नहीं है।

दीपक - कल मेरे पास आकर बाक़ी कहानी सुनाना।

कविता - ठीक है। अच्छा दीपक, अभी मैं चलती हूँ। नमस्ते।

Translate the following questions based on the conversation and then take turns with a partner to ask and answer them. Listen to the online audio and answer these questions in Hindi in the pauses provided.

1. Does Kavita tell Deepak about Eid?

2. If Deepak had gone to Lucknow, would he have celebrated Eid?

3. Do people go to the mosque and pray on the day of Eid? (*having gone to the mosque*)

4. Do you want to go to Lucknow and celebrate Eid? (*having gone to Lucknow*)

5. If Kavita were not going home, would she have told the entire story?

6. Is the story of Eid very old?

7. Which Eid did Kavita celebrate in Lucknow?

Glossary शब्दावली

The following words have appeared in the Activities that accompany Lesson 15. Most are common everyday words. Take a moment to study them along with the genders of the nouns.

अगली बार next time
अस्पताल hospital (*m*)
इम्तहान examination (*m*)
ईद-उज़-ज़ुहा name of Eid (*f*)
ईद-उल-अज़हा name of Eid (*f*)
कई several
क़रीब near
कौन-सा which
ख़राब होना to go bad, break, be spoiled (*v.i.*)
ख़ुदा God (*m*)
गाड़ी चलाना to drive a car (*v.t.*)
चाहना to want (*v.t.*)
छात्र student (*m*)
जानवर animal (*m*)
(x की) तलाश करना to search for (x) (*v.t.*)
तहज़ीब culture (*f*)

दिक़्क़त difficulty (*f*)
ध्यान देना to pay attention (*v.t.*)
नमाज़ पढ़ना to read the prayer, pray (*v.t.*)
नवाबी Nawabi, aristocratic
परीक्षा examination (*f*)
पाप sin (*m*)
पास होना to pass (an exam) (*v.i.*)
पुराना old
पूरा complete
प्याला cup (*m*)
प्यास thirst (*f*)
बंगला Bengali language (*f*)
बकरईद name of Eid (*f*)
बलिदान sacrifice (*m*)
बाकी remaining, rest
बार turn, time (*f*)
बुझना to be extinguished, quenched (*v.i.*)

बुलाना to call, invite (*v.t.*)
मतलब meaning (*m*)
मदद help (*f*)
मनाना to celebrate, persuade (*v.t.*)
मस्जिद mosque (*f*)
महत्त्वपूर्ण important
मिटना to be effaced (*v.i.*)
(x को) याद करना to remember (x) (*v.t.*)
व्याकरण grammar (*m*)
शर्बत sherbert (*m*)
शानदार glorious, splendid
शिक्षिका teacher (*f*)
(x की) समझ में आना (x) to understand (to come into x's understanding) (*v.i.*)
समय time (*m*)
सुनाना to tell, relate (a story, etc.) (*v.t.*)

LESSON **16** सोलहवाँ पाठ

My Favorite Place in Delhi

🎧 Complete the following sentences by supplying the correct form of the verb conjugated in the optative. Then translate them and listen to them on the online audio, repeating them in the pauses provided.

1. शायद मैं यह किताब _____ । (पढ़ना)

   _____

2. संभव है कि वह हिन्दी सीखकर भारत _____ । (जाना)

   _____

3. हिन्दुस्तान जा कर हम क्या _____? (करना)

   _____

4. शायद इस साल छात्र परीक्षा में अच्छा काम _____ । (करना)

   _____

5. उस की इच्छा है कि उस के सिर पर काम का बोझ न _____ । (होना)

   _____

6. मैं चाहता हूँ कि आप सभी लोग परीक्षा में सफल _____ । (होना)

   _____

7. शायद वह आप की मदद _____ । (करना)

   _____

8. जल्दी पढ़ाई ख़त्म करो ताकि तुम फ़िल्म देखने _____ । (जाना)

   _____

9. बेटे, तुम ख़ुश .... । (रहना)

_____

10. कृपया मुझे चिट्ठी लिख कर .... । (भेजना)

_____

ACTIVITY 16.2

🎧 Translate the following sentences into Hindi and then listen to them on the online audio, repeating them in the pauses provided.

1. Perhaps the teacher was talking to your friend today.

_____

2. It is possible (that) he may have finished his Hindi work.

_____

3. I think that perhaps she may have taken her (own) mother and gone to India.

_____

4. I think (that) perhaps I may have seen this film.

_____

5. Perhaps she may be speaking to the students right now.

_____

6. Perhaps they may not have eaten by now.

_____

7. Perhaps these students study in the library.

_____

8. Perhaps he has written the letter and sent it. (*having written*)

_____

9. Perhaps she goes to India every year.

_____

ACTIVITY 16.3

Conversation बातचीत

Read and translate this conversation into English and then listen to it on the online audio. Here Deepak and Kavita talk about taking a trip to Allahabad.

स्थान : दीपक का घर, नई दिल्ली
पात्र : कविता, दीपक

दीपक - हाय कविता, अंदर आओ। कैसी हो तुम?
कविता - मज़े में हूँ। तुम सुनाओ।
दीपक - बस, सब ठीक ही चल रहा है।
कविता - क्या तुम्हारे पिता जी इलाहाबाद वापस गये?
दीपक - हाँ, हाँ। वे पिछले हफ़्ते वापस गये थे। वे मुझसे कहकर गये थे कि तुम कविता को लेकर इलाहाबाद ज़रूर आना। क्या तुम कभी इलाहाबाद गयी हो?
कविता - न, मैं कभी नहीं गयी। चलो, क्या हम इलाहाबाद घूम आयें?
दीपक - हाँ, मैं तुमसे पूछना चाहता था लेकिन मैंने सोचा कि शायद इस समय तुम्हारे पास बहुत ज़्यादा काम हो।
कविता - नहीं तो। यह विचार कहाँ से आया? दो हफ़्ते पहले मेरी परीक्षा ख़त्म हुई थी। आजकल मेरे पास काफ़ी समय है।
दीपक - यह तो अच्छी बात है। क्या मैं तुम्हारे माँ-बाप से जाने की बात करूँ?
कविता - इसकी क्या ज़रूरत है? मेरे मम्मी-पापा को कोई ऐसी आपत्ति नहीं होती। शायद अभी मम्मी घर में कुछ काम कर रही हों। क्या मैं अभी फ़ोन करके पूछूँ?
दीपक - ज़रूर! तुम अभी फ़ोन करो, मैं दो कप चाय बना कर लाता हूँ।

_____

_____

_____

Translate the following questions based on the conversation and then take turns with a partner to ask and answer them. Listen to the online audio and answer these questions in Hindi in the pauses provided.

1. Has Deepak's father returned to Allahabad?

2. When had Deepak's father returned to Allahabad?

3. Has Kavita ever been to Allahabad?

4. Is it possible that Deepak and Kavita may go to Allahabad?

5. Is it possible that you may go to Allahabad?

6. What does Deepak make and bring?

7. Is it possible that you may go to Allahabad with Deepak?

Glossary शब्दावली

The following words have appeared in the Activities that accompany Lesson 16. Most are common everyday words. Take a moment to study them along with the genders of the nouns.

आपत्ति objection (*f*)

कृपया please

ख़त्म करना to finish (*v.t.*)

ख़त्म होना to be finished (*v.i.*)

ख़ुश happy

घूमना to revolve, wander (*v.i.*)

ज़रूर certainly

ज़रूरत necessity (*f*)

जल्दी quickly

ताकि so that (*conj*)

नहीं तो certainly not

पढ़ाई study (*f*)

पहले before, ago

फ़ोन phone (*m*)

फ़ोन करना to phone (*v.t.*)

बोझ burden (*m*)

भेजना to send (*v.t.*)

लाना to bring (*v.i.*)

वापस जाना to return (*v.i.*)

विचार idea, thought (*m*)

सफल successful

सम्भव possible

LESSON **17** सत्रहवाँ पाठ

How Much Is That?

🎧   Translate the following sentences and then listen to them on the online audio, repeating them in the pauses provided.

1. Next week I (*f*) will go to India. _____

2. Tomorrow we (*m*) will come (*in*)to class. _____

3. Will you (*m*) watch television tonight? _____

4. On Monday morning she will phone me. _____

5. Next year he will go to India and study Hindi. _____

6. The day after tomorrow our exam will take place. _____

7. They said that they will think about this matter. _____

8. On Tuesday I (*m*) will do nothing. _____

9. On Saturday she is going (will go) to the city to see a movie. _____

10. My friend will bring some clothes for you from India. _____

11. हम शराब नहीं पिएँगे। _____

12. काम पूरा करके ही तुम जाओगे। _____

13. वह सामान अपने यहाँ से ले कर मेरे घर आयेगी, न? _____

14. मैं आपकी घड़ी ठीक करने के लिये घड़ीसाज़ को दूँगा। _____

15. दो हफ़्ते बाद हमारी कक्षा होगी या नहीं? _____

16. तू भविष्य में मेरी मदद करेगी? _____

17. शायद वह हिन्दुस्तान से आपको पत्र लिखेगा। _____

18. अगले हफ़्ते कचहरी में सुनवाही होगी। _____

19. कल हम इस की बात फ़ोन पर करेंगे। _____

20. आप लोग बहुत मेहनत करके ही परीक्षा में सफल होंगे। _____

ACTIVITY 17.2

🎧 Translate the following sentences and then listen to them on the online audio, repeating them in the pauses provided.

1. She must be working in her room. _____

2. Deepak must be coming to university right now. (*must come*) _____

3. This must/will be right as well. _____

4. He must have finished his work by now. _____

5. They will be studying Hindi in the library right now. _____

6. You (*m*) must rise by six o'clock. (तुम) _____

7. Perhaps he has not gone by now. (*must not have gone*) _____

8. This must be expensive. (*the price of this must be a lot*) _____

9. The students must speak in Hindi to their teacher. (not an obligation)

_____

10. That must have taken place ten years ago. _____

11. सोमवार को उनकी कक्षा होती होगी। _____

12. मंगलवार को वह विश्वविद्यालय जाती होगी। _____

13. बुध को यह घटना हुई होगी। _____

14. बृहस्पति को सब छात्र भारत गये होंगे। _____

15. उसे दिक़ मत करना। वह कुछ काम कर रही होगी। _____

ACTIVITY 17.3

🎧 Complete the sentences supplying the appropriate form of the verb, following the example. Then translate them into English and listen to them on the online audio, repeating them in the pauses provided.

कल पिता जी ने मुझे फ़िल्म देखने नहीं जाने दिया। (जाना to go + देना)
Yesterday my father wouldn't let me go and see a film.

1. (तुम) उसे हिन्दुस्तान का सफ़र _____ । (करना to do + देना) imperative

_____

2. देखना कि चोर न _____ । (भागना to flee + पाना) optative

_____

3. मेरी ओर देखकर वह (f) फ़ोन _____ । (रखना to place, keep + लगना) past

_____

4. फ़िल्म देख कर हम (m) अपने बारे में _____ । (सोचना to think + लगना) past

_____

5. (आप) उन्हें यहाँ _____ । (बैठना to sit + देना) optative

_____

🎧 Translate the following sentences into Hindi and then listen to them on the online audio, repeating them in the pauses provided.

6. Perhaps I may allow you to go to India and learn Hindi. _____

_____

7. He opened the door and began to come inside. _____

_____

8. On Monday we will begin to read a new story. _____

_____

9. There's no way she will be able take her mother (and go) to India. (*having taken her own mother she will not be able to go...*)

_____

10. They stood up and began to give a speech amongst all the people.

ACTIVITY 17.4

🎧 Translate the following sentences and then listen to them on the online audio, repeating them in the pauses provided.

1. अगर आप विश्वविद्यालय आयें तो मुझसे मिलिये।

2. यहाँ मोची कहाँ मिलेगा?

3. हर महीने तुम्हें कितने पैसे मिलते हैं?

4. जनपथ राजपथ से मिलता है।*
   * The names of two major roads in Delhi.

5. शायद मैं आप से कभी मिली होऊँ।

6. पिछले हफ़्ते उसे शहर में अपनी दोस्त मिली थी।

7. अगर मुझे नौकरी मिले तो बहुत अच्छा होगा।

ACTIVITY 17.5

Conversation बातचीत

🎧 Read and translate this conversation into English and then listen to it on the online audio. Here Deepak and Kavita arrive in Allahabad at Deepak's parents' house.

स्थान : दीपक का घर, इलाहाबाद
पात्र : कविता, दीपक, दीपक की माँ विमला

दीपक — माँ, पिता जी कहाँ हैं?
दीपक की माँ — वे तो कुछ सामान लेने बाज़ार गये हैं।
दीपक — माँ, क्या आप कविता से कभी मिलीं?
दीपक की माँ — शायद हम मिले हों। तुम कहाँ रहती हो, बेटी?
कविता — जी, मैं दिल्ली में रहती हूँ। आप कभी दिल्ली गयीं?
दीपक की माँ — नहीं बेटी।
कविता — तब तो हम पहले कभी नहीं मिले होंगे क्योंकि मैं इससे पहले कभी इलाहाबाद नहीं आयी।

दीपक की माँ	- तुम दीपक के साथ पढ़ती होगी, न?
कविता	- जी हाँ, लेकिन अगले साल से मैं डॉक्टरी की पढ़ाई करूँगी। मैं बच्चों का इलाज करना चाहती हूँ।
दीपक की माँ	- वह तो अच्छा होगा। दीपक तुम पढ़कर पत्रकार बनोगे, न?
दीपक	- बनने की कोशिश करूँगा। मैं कुछ लेख लिखने भी लगा हूँ। मेरा एक लेख अख़बार में छपा भी था।
दीपक की माँ	- बहुत अच्छा। तुम दोनों बैठक में जाकर बैठो। मैं चाय बनाकर पिलाती हूँ। तुम्हारे पिता जी अभी आते होंगे।
कविता	- इलाहाबाद में देखने को क्या मिलता है?
दीपक की माँ	- संगम तो है। तुमने उसके बारे में सुना होगा। दीपक के पिता जी तुम दोनों को दिखाने के लिये ले जाएँगे।
कविता	- क्या हम गंगा में नहाने भी पायेंगे?
दीपक की माँ	- अगर तुम नहाना चाहती हो तो ज़रूर। लेकिन पानी बहुत ठंडा होगा।

_____

Translate the following questions based on the conversation and then take turns with a partner to ask and answer them. Listen to the online audio and answer these questions in Hindi in the pauses provided.

1. Have Deepak and Kavita gone to Allahabad?

2. Why has Deepak's father gone to the market?

3. Must Kavita have met Deepak's mother previously?

4. Must Kavita study with Deepak?

5. Has Deepak begun writing stories?

6. Have you ever met (with) Deepak's parents?

7. Will you go to Allahabad and meet (with) Deepak's parents? (yes) (*having gone*)

8. Will Deepak and Kavita go into the living room and drink tea? (yes)

9. Must the water in the River Ganges be very cold these days?

Glossary शब्दावली

The following words have appeared in the Activities that accompany Lesson 17. Most are common everyday words. Take a moment to study them along with the genders of the nouns.

अध्यापक lecturer (*m*)

कचहरी court (*f*)

x की ओर in the direction of x

x से/के पहले before x

x के बीच में amongst x

x के यहाँ at x's place

खोलना to open (*v.t.*)

घड़ीसाज़ watchmaker (*m*)

चोर thief (*m*)

छपना to be published (*v.i.*)

छै बजे at six o'clock

ठीक करना to fix (*v.t.*)

दरवाज़ा door (*m*)

दिक् करना to harass, trouble (*v.t.*)

दो हफ़्ते बाद after two weeks

नाटक play (*m*)

नौकरी employment (*f*)

परसों the day before yesterday/ day after tomorrow

पहले previously

पहुँचना to arrive (*v.i.*)

बच्चा child (*m*)

बैठक sitting room (*f*)

भविष्य future (*m*)

भागना to escape (*v.i.*)

भाषण देना to give a speech (*v.t.*)

मिलना to meet (*v.i.*)

मेहनत करना to work hard (*v.t.*)

मोची cobbler (*m*)

या or (*conj*)

रखना to keep, place (*v.t.*)

लाना to bring (*v.i.*)

लेख article (*m*)

लेखक author (*m*)

सफ़र करना to travel (*v.t.*)

सफल होना to be successful (*v.i.*)

सुनवाई hearing (*f*)

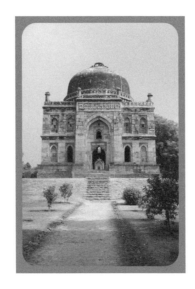

LESSON **18** अठारहवाँ पाठ

What Do You Like?

🎧 Translate the following sentences and then listen to them on the online audio, repeating them in the pauses provided.

1. उन्हें काफ़ी गुस्सा आता होगा। _____

2. लेकिन ऐसा भी लगता है कि उन्हें डर भी बहुत लगता है। _____

3. पर मुझे आशा है कि एक दिन उन्हें शांति मिलेगी। _____

4. क्योंकि अगर उन्हें शान्ति नहीं मिली तो बहुत परेशान रहेंगे। _____

   _____

5. आप को ज़िंदगी की असलियत मालूम होगी। _____

6. कल ही मुझे पता चला कि भारत जाने में बहुत पैसे लगते हैं। _____

   _____

7. लेकिन वहाँ जाना आपको पसंद होगा। _____

8. किसको हिन्दी आती है? _____

9. मुझे ज़ोर की भूख लगी है। _____

10. शायद बस से न्यू यार्क जाने में चार घंटे लगते हों। _____

11. It (such) must seem to you that I do not like to eat fruit. _____

12. He/she really used to like to read Hindi books in the library. _____

13. It seems to me that you must not have any money. _____

14. Medha really enjoys drinking tea. _____

15. It takes only twenty minutes to write a letter. _____

ACTIVITY 18.2

🎧 Translate the sentences following the example. Then listen to them on the online audio, repeating them in the pauses provided.

It took two years to find out.　　　पता चलने में दो साल लगे।

1. It takes me a week to finish one lesson.

2. It must take two days to go to India by plane.

3. It has begun to take forty minutes to reach his house from the city.

4. It will take a long time (delay) to discover the truth.

5. It takes some years to learn another language.

6. It may take a lot of money to go to India.

7. It takes enough hard work to knead dough (flour).

ACTIVITY 18.3

🎧 Answer the following questions in Hindi. Then listen to them on the online audio, repeating them in the pauses provided.

1. कल दोपहर को साढ़े तीन बजे आप क्या कर रहे थे? (कर रही थीं)

2. कल क्या आप दोपहर को पौन बजे मेरे घर आएँगे? (आएँगी)

3. कल ढाई बजे क्या आप किताब पढ़ रहे थे? (पढ़ रही थीं)

_____

4. क्या तुम रोज़ दोपहर को डेढ़ बजे दिन का खाना खाते हो? (खाती हो)

_____

5. आज सुबह सवा दस बजे तक क्या तुम सोये थे? (सोयी थीं)

_____

ACTIVITY 18.4

Conversation बातचीत

Read and translate this conversation into English and then listen to it on the online audio. Here Deepak and Kavita discuss going to see a film on the weekend.

स्थान : दिल्ली विश्वविद्यालय, नई दिल्ली
पात्र : कविता, दीपक

दीपक - नमस्ते कविता, तुम अभी क्या कर रही हो?
कविता - क्लास में जा रही हूँ। कितने बजे हैं?
दीपक - अभी ढाई बजे हैं। क्या तुम्हें मालूम है कि एक नयी फ़िल्म लगी है?
कविता - नहीं, मुझे मालूम नहीं था। क्या नाम है उसका?
दीपक - "मैं भी हूँ, न"। देखने को चलोगी?
कविता - शायद मैं चलूँ। तुम किस दिन और कितने बजे चलोगे?
दीपक - मैं कुछ दोस्तों के साथ शनिवार को शाम के छै बजे का शो देखने जाऊँगा।
कविता - सोचूँगी। मुझे ऐसी फ़िल्में इतनी अच्छी नहीं लगतीं।
दीपक - कैसे मालूम है कि फ़िल्म अच्छी नहीं होगी। मैंने सुना कि बहुत अच्छी है।
कविता - ठीक है। मुझे बहुत भूख लगी है। क्लास से पहले चाय पीने को मेरे साथ चलोगे?
दीपक - मुझे यहाँ की चाय अच्छी नहीं लगती। लेकिन यहाँ की कॉफ़ी मुझे पसंद है। तो कॉफ़ी पियूँगा। क्या तुमने दिन में कुछ खाना नहीं खाया?
कविता - मेरे पास वक़्त नहीं था। बारह बजे मेरी एक क्लास होती है। और सवेरे कॉलेज आने में मुझे पूरे दो घंटे लगते हैं। हमेशा मुझे आने में देर होती है।
दीपक - अच्छा, तो शनिवार को फ़िल्म देखने चलोगी या नहीं।
कविता - ठीक है, बाबा। चलूँगी। कब और कहाँ मिलेंगे?
दीपक - शाम को साढ़े चार बजे मेरे घर आना। वहाँ से चलेंगे।
कविता - अच्छा अब मैं क्लास में जा रही हूँ। शनिवार को मिलेंगे।

🎧 Translate the following questions based on the conversation and then take turns with a partner to ask and answer them. Listen to the online audio and answer these questions in Hindi in the pauses provided.

1. What is Kavita doing right now?

2. Does Kavita know that a new film has come out?

3. On which day and at what time will Deepak go to watch (for watching) the film?

4. Will Deepak go to watch the film with some friends?

5. Does Kavita like such films?

6. Do you like Hindi('s) films?

7. Does Deepak like the tea here?

8. Do you like tea or coffee?

9. Do you have a class at 12 P.M.?

10. Do you want to go to see a film?

Glossary शब्दावली

The following words have appeared in the Activities that accompany Lesson 18. Most are common everyday words. Take a moment to study them along with the genders of the nouns.

(x को) अच्छा लगना (x) to like (*v.i.*)

असलियत reality (*f*)

आटा flour (*m*)

(x को) आशा होना (x) to hope (*v.i.*)

(x को) गुस्सा आना (x) to become angry (*v.i.*)

गूँधना to knead (*v.t.*)

चालीस forty

ज़रा a little (also used to soften a request)

जीवन life (*m*)

(x को) डर लगना (x) to feel afraid (*v.i.*)

ढाई two and a half

देर delay, lateness (*f*)

(x को) पता चलना (x) to find out (*v.i.*)

परेशान troubled, bothered

(x को) पसंद होना (x) to enjoy (*v.i.*)

पाठ lesson, reading (*m*)

फल fruit (*m*)

बजना to strike (*v.i.*)

(x को) भूख लगना (x) to feel hungry (*v.i.*)

(x को) मालूम होना to be known (to x) (*v.i.*)

मेहनत hard work, industry (*f*)

(x को) लगना to attach, to seem (to x) (*v.i.*)

वक़्त time (*m*)

शांति peace (*f*)

सच्चाई truth (*f*)

हवाई जहाज़ plane (*m*)

I Want to Leave at Five-Thirty

ACTIVITY 19.1

Following the information given, answer the questions in Hindi. Then listen to the online audio, repeating your answers in the pauses provided.

1. क्या तुम कल रात मेरी पार्टी में आओगे? (f - आओगी)
   No, I will not be able to come. (आ पाना) ....

2. क्या तुमने "ॐ शान्ति ॐ" फ़िल्म देखी है?
   Yes, I have already seen that film. (देख चुकना) ....

3. क्या तुम हिन्दी बोल भी सकते हो? (f - सकती हो)
   Yes, I can also speak Hindi. (बोल सकना) ....

4. क्या कल शाम तक यह काम ख़त्म होगा?
   This work will already have happened by midday tomorrow. (हो चुकना)* ....
   * Use the presumptive (future form of होना here with हो चुकना. See Textbook p. 161.)

5. क्या तुम्हारा दोस्त गाड़ी चलाना सीखेगा?
   Yes, he will be able to learn to drive a car. (सीख सकना) ....

6. क्या तुम्हारे भाई ने तुम्हें हिन्दुस्तान जाने के पैसे दिये?
   No, he was not able to give me the money to go to India. (दे पाना) ....

7. क्या तुम्हारे दोस्त की बहन कॉलेज में पढ़ाई कर रही है?
   No, her studies are already complete. (हो चुकना) ....

ACTIVITY 19.2

Complete the passage by inserting the most appropriate verb from those listed below. Then translate the passage and listen to it on the online audio.

मेट्रो में एक मुलाक़ात

कल एक बजे मैं मेट्रो से दिल्ली यूनिवर्सिटी जा रही थी। मेरे हाथ में तीन किताबें थीं। राजीव चौक के स्टेशन पर गाड़ी के दरवाज़े खुले और अचानक दीपक मेरे सामने आ खड़ा _____। बग़ल की कुर्सी ख़ाली थी। मैंने कहा कि "यहाँ _____।" फिर मैंने पूछा कि "क्या तुमने दिन का खाना _____?" दीपक ने जवाब दिया कि "हाँ, मैं खाना _____।" मैंने कहा कि "अगर तुमने खाना नहीं खाया होता तो मैं तुम्हें खाना _____।" थोड़ी देर बाद उसने कहा "क्या तुम्हें अच्छी अंग्रेज़ी आती है?" मैंने कहा कि "हाँ, क्यों?" उसने मुझसे पूछा कि "क्या तुम मुझे अंग्रेज़ी _____?" मैंने हँसकर कहा कि "हाँ। अगर तुम मुझसे अंग्रेज़ी _____ तो मैं तुम्हें अंग्रेज़ी _____।" दीपक दूसरी ओर देखकर _____। फिर मैंने दीपक को एक अंग्रेज़ी की किताब _____ और कहा कि "आज शाम को मेरे घर आना। मैं माँ से _____ कि तुम खाना खाने आ रहे हो।" उस के बाद बहाना बनाकर अचानक दीपक उठा और पुरानी दिल्ली स्टेशन पर _____। मुझे ज़ोर की हँसी _____।

मुस्करा देना (perfective tense)	खा लेना (perfective tense)	दे देना (perfective tense)
बैठ जाना (imperative)	सिखा देना (future)	कह देना (future)
सीख पाना (optative)	खा चुकना (perfective tense)	आ पड़ना (perfective tense)
उतर जाना (perfective tense)	खिला देना (contrary to fact)	
हो जाना (perfective tense)	सिखा सकना (imperfect present)	

ACTIVITY 19.3

🎧 Translate the following sentences and then listen to them on the online audio, repeating them in the pauses provided.

1. I am taller than you. _____

2. You are older than my brother. (तुम) _____

3. Hindi is easier than English. _____

4. The seventh lesson must be the most difficult. _____

5. She is the youngest in the family. _____

6. That film is a bit better than this film. (a bit = थोड़ा) _____

7. Bombay is a bigger city than Delhi. _____

8. Give me the thickest book from amongst those books.
   (Use a compound verb: to give *for the benefit of someone else*)

ACTIVITY 19.4

Conversation बातचीत

🎧 Read and translate this conversation into English and then listen to it on the online audio. Here Kavita and Deepak talk about celebrating the festival of colors, Holi.

स्थान : कविता का घर, नई दिल्ली
पात्र : कविता, दीपक

कविता – दीपक, इस साल तुम होली मनाने इलाहाबाद वापस जाओगे?

दीपक – मेरे ख़्याल में मैं जा नहीं पाऊँगा। उस समय इम्तहान सिर पर होंगे।

कविता – तो हमारे यहाँ खेलने के लिये आ जाना। बहुत मज़ा आएगा। हम धूमधाम से सब त्यौहार मनाते हैं। कुछ दिन बाद मेरे भाई भी आस्ट्रेलिया से आएँगे। सब सामान, गुलाल, पिचकारी, वग़ैरह भी घर में आ गया है। सब तैयारियाँ हो चुकी हैं।

दीपक – मुझे होली का त्यौहार सब से अच्छा लगता है।

कविता – कॉलेज से दो-एक और दोस्त भी आएँगे। तुम्हारे पास पुराने कपड़े तो हैं, न?

दीपक – मेरे पास नये कपड़े कहाँ हैं? मेरे सब कपड़े पुराने हैं।

कविता – वह तो है। तो उस दिन सब से पुराने कपड़े पहनकर आना। याद रखना, हम खेलने में किसी से भी कम नहीं हैं। डटकर खेलते हैं।

दीपक – ठीक है, हम तैयार रहेंगे।* तुम फ़िक्र मत करो। हम भी किसी से कम नहीं हैं।

---

* Here Deepak is using the first person plural pronoun to talk about himself. This usage is common in Hindi and in most contexts understood as more self-effacing.

कविता - पिछले साल रंग उतरने में पूरा एक हफ़्ता लगा था।

दीपक - तुम लोग गुझिया* भी बनाते हो?

कविता - और क्या। लेकिन सावधान रहना। मेरे भाई सब गुझिया खा जाएँगे।

दीपक - ठीक है। तो होली के दिन कितने बजे तुम्हारे घर आऊँ?

कविता - रात को यहीं रहना। बाक़ी दोस्त भी रहेंगे। हम सुबह सुबह खेलना शुरू करेंगे, इसलिये।

* Gujhiya is a sweet made from refined flour, filled with boiled down milk solids, semolina, raisins, cashews and sugar and then fried in clarified butter.

Translate the following questions based on the conversation and then take turns with a partner to ask and answer them. Listen to the online audio and answer these questions in Hindi in the pauses provided.

1. Will Deepak be able to go home to celebrate Holi this year?

2. Will you be able to go to India to celebrate Holi this year?

3. Will Kavita's brother come from Australia to celebrate Holi?

4. Have all of the preparations for Holi already taken place? (*Holi's preparations*)

5. Does Deepak like Holi most of all?

6. Which festival do you like most of all? (कौन-सा which)

7. Do people wear new clothes and play Holi? (*having worn new clothes…*)

8. Last year how many days did it take Kavita to wash out the Holi color?

9. Will Kavita's brother eat up all of the gujhiya?

Glossary शब्दावली

The following words have appeared in the Activities that accompany Lesson 19. Most are common everyday words. Take a moment to study them along with the genders of the nouns.

अचानक suddenly

इम्तहान examination (*m*)

उतरना to descend, to come off (*v.i.*)

ख़्याल thought, opinion (*m*)

गुझिया gujhiya, a type of Indian sweet (*f*)

गुलाल colored powder thrown at the time of Holi (*m*)

डटकर having taken a stand, resolutely

तैयारी preparation (*f*)

थोड़ी देर बाद after a little while

दोपहर midday (*f*)

धूमधाम pomp, fanfare (*f*)

पढ़ाई studies (*f*)

पिचकारी water gun, syringe (*f*)

पूरा होना to be completed (*v.i.*)

फ़िक्र worry (*f*)

(x की) फ़िक्र करना to worry (about x) (*v.t.*)

बग़ल flank, armpit, next to (*f*)

बम्बई Bombay (*f*)

बहाना excuse (*m*)

बहाना बनाना to make an excuse (*v.t.*)

बाक़ी rest, remaining, remainder

मज़ा आना to be enjoyable (*v.i.*)

मनाना to appease, celebrate (*v.t.*)

मुलाक़ात meeting (*f*)

मुस्कराना to smile (*v.i.*)

मोटा fat

याद रखना to keep in mind (*v.t.*)

रंग color (*m*)

लम्बा tall

वग़ैरह etcetera

वापस जाना to return (*v.i.*)

शुरू करना to begin (*v.t.*)

सच true

सावधान रहना to remain vigilant (*v.i.*)

सिर पर होना to be on the head (to be imminent) (*v.i.*)

होली festival of colors to herald the coming of spring (*f*)

होली खेलना to play Holi (*v.t.*)

LESSON **20** बीसवाँ पाठ

I Can't Come on Tuesday

🎧 Translate the following sentences. Then listen to them on the online audio, repeating them in the pauses provided.

1. Do you have to drink tea? ....

2. I should go to India to learn Hindi. ....

3. Kavita should have spoken more about herself. (use अपना) ....

....

4. We must sit/take our Hindi exam in May. (to sit/take an exam = *to give* an exam)

....

5. He has to/wants to read this book. ....

6. शायद अगले साल मुझे और किराया देना पड़े। ....

7. विद्यार्थियों को अपना काम करके ही क्लास में आना चाहिये। ....

....

8. किसी को शराब पीकर गाड़ी चलानी नहीं चाहिए। ....

....

9. इस साल के अंत में सब लोगों को लखनऊ जाना ही पड़ेगा। ....

....

10. तुम्हें यह किताबें ख़रीदनी चाहिये थीं। ....

....

ACTIVITY 20.2

🎧 Translate the following sentences. Then listen to them on the online audio, repeating them in the pauses provided.

1. Our train was about to depart. ....

2. Call the tall boy. (use वाला) ....

3. There are thirty students of Hindi this year. (*Hindi learners*) ....

....

4. I am about to smoke a cigarette. ....

5. I am a cigarette smoker. ....

6. I live in Delhi (*I am a liver of Delhi*) ....

7. He is about to eat meat. ....

8. He is a meat eater. ....

9. They were about to read this book. ....

10. Bring the book with the green cover. ....

11. इस साल के अंत में कितने लोग भारत जानेवाले हैं? ....

....

12. शायद बारिश होनेवाली हो। ....

13. मुझे अपना लाल वाला स्वेटर दे दो। ....

14. चायवाले से कह दो कि इससे तेज़ चाय बना दे। ....

....

15. मैं विश्वविद्यालय जाने को हूँ। ....

ACTIVITY 20.3

Conversation बातचीत

🎧 Read and translate this conversation into English and then listen to it on the online audio. Here Kavita tells Deepak about her plans for the future.

स्थान : दीपक का घर, नई दिल्ली

पात्र : कविता, दीपक

दीपक – नमस्ते कविता, तुम यहाँ कैसे आ गयीं?

कविता – ऐसे ही। यहाँ से गुज़र रही थी। तो सोचा कि पाँच मिनट के लिये तुमसे मिल लूँगी। क्या कर रहे हो अभी?

दीपक – कुछ नहीं। चाय पीनेवाला था। तुम्हारे लिये मैं चाय बनवा दूँ?

कविता – हाँ, मुझे चाय की तलब लगी तो है।

दीपक – तेज़ वाली चाय बनवा दूँ या हल्की वाली चाय?

कविता – मुझे तेज़ वाली अच्छी लगती है। क्या वृन्दा यहाँ है?

दीपक – नहीं। कल ही उसे इलाहाबाद वापस जाना पड़ा। सिर्फ़ दो हफ़्ते के लिये आ सकी। कविता, इस महीने के अंत में पढ़ाई पूरी हो जाने पर तुम क्या करनेवाली हो?

कविता – मेरी इच्छा है कि मैं चिकित्सा पढ़ना शुरू करने से पहले दुनिया देखने जा पाऊँ।

दीपक – अच्छा, कहाँ-कहाँ जाओगी?

कविता – मुझे अपने भाई से मिलने के लिये ऑस्ट्रेलिया जाना होगा। वहाँ मैं देखना चाहती हूँ कि ऑस्ट्रेलिया कैसी जगह है। अगर मुझे अच्छा लगा तो शायद मैं वहाँ आगे पढ़ने के बारे में सोचूँगी। या शायद अमरीका की राह पकड़ूँ।

दीपक – अच्छा, चाय बन गयी है। ले लो। क्या तुम शादी के बारे में कभी नहीं सोचतीं?

कविता – अरे! मेरे पास शादी के लिये वक्त कहाँ है? मुझे ज़िंदगी में बहुत कुछ करना है। नौकरी, घूमना, अपना कैरियर बनाना, यह सब कुछ मुझे करना है।

दीपक – वह तो ठीक है लेकिन शादी भी अपनी जगह बुरी चीज़ नहीं है।

कविता – अगर कोई अच्छा आदमी, यानी अच्छा "जीवन साथी" मिल जाए, तब।

दीपक – अभी तक कोई नहीं मिला क्या?

कविता – शायद दो-एक विकल्प हों। ओह, पाँच बज चुके हैं, मुझे घर जाना चाहिये।

दीपक – इतनी जल्दी? तुम अभी तो आयी हो।

कविता – हाँ, लेकिन सचमुच मुझे जाना ही पड़ेगा। माँ का कुछ काम करने इस तरफ़ आयी थी।

दीपक – अच्छा, मैं नयी फ़िल्म की डी० वी० डी० लाया हूँ। अगर तुम्हें फ़िल्म देखनी हो तो कल आना।

कविता – ठीक है, शायद मैं आऊँगी कल। कितने बजे?

दीपक – शाम को किसी भी समय आना। अच्छा, कल मिलेंगे।

_____

_____

_____

_____

_____

_____

_____

_____

_____

_____

_____

_____

🎧 Translate the following questions based on the conversation and then take turns with a partner to ask and answer them. Listen to the online audio and answer these questions in Hindi in the pauses provided.

1. Does Kavita want to marry soon? _____

2. In your opinion, does Deepak want to marry Kavita? _____

3. Does Kavita want to drink tea? (*does Kavita have to drink tea*) _____

4. Do you want to drink tea right now? _____

5. Do you like strong or weak tea? _____

6. Having finished your studies, do you want to see the world? _____

7. Are you going to work after finishing your studies? (*having finished*) ....

....

8. Is there a lot you want to do in life? (*in life do you have to do much*) ....

....

9. Do you have to go home and cook tonight? (*having gone home will you have to cook*) ....

....

Glossary शब्दावली

The following words have appeared in the Activities that accompany Lesson 20. Most are common everyday words. Take a moment to study them along with the genders of the nouns.

इच्छा desire (*f*)

गुज़रना to pass (by) (*v.i.*)

गोश्त meat, flesh (*m*)

चिकित्सा medical treatment, remedy, medicine (*f*)

छूटना to depart, be released (*v.i.*)

जल्दी quickly, soon

ज़िंदगी life (*f*)

जिल्द cover, binding (*f*)

जीवन साथी life companion (*m*)

तलब yearning, desire (*f*)

तेज़ sharp, strong, harsh

नौकरी work (*f*)

नौकरी करना to work (*v.t.*)

पकड़ना to grab, catch (*v.t.*)

परीक्षा देना to sit an exam (*v.t.*)

बारिश rain (*f*)

राह way, path (*f*)

लाना to bring (*v.i.*)

विकल्प alternative, option (*m*)

विद्यार्थी student (*m*)

शादी करना to marry (*v.t.*)

(x से) शादी करना to marry (x) (*v.t.*)

सिगरेट पीना to smoke a cigarette (*v.t.*)

हल्का light (not heavy), weak

LESSON 21 इक्कीसवाँ पाठ

Forgive Me, I Was Delayed

ACTIVITY 21.1

🎧 Transform the following sentences from the active voice into the passive and then translate them. Then listen to them on the online audio, repeating them in the pauses provided.

1. मैंने यह किताब पढ़ ली। ....

....

2. आपने हम सभी लोगों के लिये टिकट ख़रीदे होंगे। ....

....

3. हारवर्ड यूनिवर्सिटी में लोग हिन्दी सीखते हैं। ....

....

4. उत्तर प्रदेश में लोग हिन्दी बोलते हैं। ....

....

5. पुलिस ने चोर को गिरफ़्तार कर लिया। ....

....

6. सरकार ने एक नया क़ानून बनाया है। ....

....

7. कहते हैं कि पाकिस्तान से हिन्दुस्तान में ज़्यादा लोग उर्दू बोलते हैं। ....

....

8. शादी के लिये बावर्ची ने शानदार खाने की चीज़ें तैयार कीं। ....

....

9. अगर अपना काम तुम लोग ठीक समय पर दे देते तो... ।

10. हम यह सब खाना खा गये ।

ACTIVITY 21.2

🎧 Translate the following sentences into Hindi, using the passive of inability. Then listen to them on the online audio, repeating them in the pauses provided.

1. Last night I could not sleep.

2. She was unable to read this book.

3. He will not be able to make the rice.

4. I cannot bear to watch this movie.

5. We are not able to drink the water in India.

6. They cannot eat such spicy food.

7. In Lucknow the students will not be able to study six hours a day.

8. Sanskrit is so difficult that I cannot learn it.

ACTIVITY 21.3

Conversation बातचीत

Read and translate this conversation into English and then listen to it on the online audio. Here Deepak runs into Kavita on the street on her way to the pharmacy.

स्थान : सड़क में, नई दिल्ली
पात्र : कविता, दीपक

दीपक - नमस्ते कविता, तुम्हें इतनी जल्दी क्यों? कहाँ जा रही हो तुम?
कविता - अरे दीपक, नमस्ते। मुझे अभी दवाख़ाने में जाना है। काफ़ी जरूरी काम है।
दीपक - क्यों? क्या हुआ? कोई बीमार तो नहीं हो गया?
कविता - हाँ, मेरी माँ काफ़ी बीमार हो गयी हैं। कल सवेरे उनसे उठा नहीं गया। डॉक्टर को भी बुलाया गया। और फिर उन्होंने ख़ून की जाँच कराने के लिये कहा। ख़ून की जाँच कल ही करायी गयी। उस के बाद डॉक्टर परचे पर दवाई लिखकर चले गये। मैं दवाख़ाने में दवाएँ लेने जा रही हूँ।
दीपक - डॉक्टर ने कुछ और नहीं बताया?
कविता - हमें बताया गया कि माँ के पेट में कोई इन्फ़ेक्शन हो गया है। और उन्हें बहुत खाँसी भी हो रही है। उनसे रात भर सोया नहीं गया।
दीपक - तुम्हारी माँ को अस्पताल ले जाया गया या नहीं?
कविता - नहीं। अभी तो वे घर पर ही हैं। उम्मीद है कि जाने की ज़रूरत नहीं होगी।
दीपक - क्या मैं तुम्हारी कुछ मदद कर सकता हूँ?
कविता - थैंक्यू, अभी नहीं। शायद एक दो दिन के बाद बीमारी से पिंड छूट जाएगा।
दीपक - चलो। मैं तुम्हारे साथ दवा लेकर उनको देखने के लिये चलता हूँ।
कविता - ठीक है। दवाख़ाना बहुत पास है। पाँच मिनट भी नहीं लगेंगे।

_____

_____

_____

_____

_____

_____

_____

_____

_____

Translate the following questions based on the conversation and then take turns with a partner to ask and answer them. Listen to the online audio and answer these questions in Hindi in the pauses provided.

1. Who has become ill? (use हो जाना) _____

_____

2. Where does Kavita have to go? _____

_____

3. Does Kavita bump into Deepak on the street? (use मिलना) _____

_____

4. Was the doctor called? _____

_____

5. Have you got a cough at the moment? (use the progressive aspect) _____

_____

6. Does Deepak want to help Kavita? (*do Kavita's help*) _____

_____

7. Was Kavita's mother unable to sleep the entire night? (use passive of inability) ____

_____

8. Has Kavita's mother been taken to the hospital? _____

_____

Glossary शब्दावली

The following words have appeared in the Activities that accompany Lesson 21. Most are common everyday words. Take a moment to study them along with the genders of the nouns.

अस्पताल hospital (*m*)

इतना so, so much, this much

उत्तर प्रदेश Uttar Pradesh
 (a state in north India) (*m*)

उम्मीद hope, expectation (*f*)

उर्दू Urdu (*f*)

क़ानून law, regulation (*m*)

x के बाद after x

ख़ाँसी cough (*f*)

ख़ून blood (*m*)

गिरफ़्तार arrested, seized

चला जाना to move away (*v.i.*)

चावल rice (*m*)

ज़रूरी necessary

जाँच investigation (*f*)

जाँच कराना to make (someone)
 investigate (*v.t.*)

तीखा spicy, sharp

तैयार करना to prepare (*v.t.*)

दवा medicine (*f*)

(x से) पिंड छूटना to be freed (from x) (*v.i.*)

पेट stomach (*m*)

बावर्ची cook (*m*)

बीमार ill, sick

बीमारी illness (*f*)

शानदार grand, glorious

संस्कृत Sanskrit (*f*), refined

दवाई medicine (*f*)

दवाख़ाना pharmacy (*m*)

परचा chit, note, prescription (*m*)

LESSON **22** बाईसवाँ पाठ

Do You Know Urdu?

Complete the following sentences by inserting the appropriate form of the verb in parentheses (either the imperfect or the perfect participle or the oblique infinite). Then translate them and listen to them on the online audio, repeating them in the pauses provided.

1. हम हिन्दी .... रहेंगे। (सीखना to learn)

   ....

2. तुम रोज़ कम से कम दो घंटे पढ़ाई .... करो। (करना to do)

   ....

3. क्या आपसे भिखारियों की ओर .... नहीं बनता? (देखना to look/see)

   ....

4. शायद वह हर साल भारत .... करे। (जाना to go)

   ....

5. उस लड़की की तनख़्वाह .... ही जा रही थी। (बढ़ना to increase)

   ....

6. वे दोनों अभी अभी .... गये। (चलना to move)

   ....

7. मुझे पैसे .... रहना। (देना to give)

   ....

8. ये लोग तस्वीरें .... जाते हैं। (खींचना to take [photos], to pull/draw)

   ....

9. उसे दो दिन तक बिस्तर पर _____ रहना पड़ा। (लेटना to lie)

10. हमारा दोस्त भाषण _____ जाता है। (देना to give)

ACTIVITY 22.2

🎧 Translate the following sentences into Hindi, employing either the imperfect or perfect participle + रहना to give a sense of the continuation of a state. Then listen to them on the online audio, repeating them in the pauses provided.

1. He remained seated in the library all day. _____

2. I study Hindi all day. _____

3. We think about the future all the time. _____

4. I miss you greatly (*your memory constantly comes to me*) _____

5. I remained standing in the bus for two hours. _____
   (खड़ा रहना to remain standing)

ACTIVITY 22.3

🎧 Translate the sentences using the perfect participle + करना to give a sense of an action that takes place as a habit. Then listen to them on the online audio, repeating them in the pauses provided.

1. Go to (near) your (own) parents every week. _____

2. They see films regularly. (*often*) _____

3. She reads a book a day (*every day*). _____

4. A bookstore used to be on this corner. (use होना) _____

5. We will continue to travel to India. (*India journey to do*) _____

ACTIVITY 22.4

Conversation बातचीत

🎧 Read and translate this conversation into English and then listen to it on the online audio. Here Deepak and Kavita discuss the pace of change in cities like New Delhi.

स्थान : कोई कैफ़े, नई दिल्ली
पात्र : कविता, दीपक

कविता – आओ, दीपक। बैठो। तुम्हारा ही इंतज़ार कर रही थी। क्या पियोगे, कोल्ड कॉफ़ी, कॉफ़ी, मिल्क शेक, चाय?

दीपक – सिर्फ़ चाय।

कविता – बस चाय? मैं पैसे दे रही हूँ। कुछ और तो ले लो।

दीपक – बस चाय चलेगी। और कुछ पीने का मन नहीं हो रहा है।

कविता – ठीक है, बाबा। तुम्हारी मर्ज़ी। आज किस सोच में पड़ गये हो?

दीपक – क्या बताऊँ? क्या तुम कभी सोचती हो कि हमारी ज़िंदगी कितनी तेज़ी से बदलती जा रही है?

कविता – हाँ, इस बारे में सोचती रहती हूँ। ज़िंदगी की रफ़्तार बहुत तेज़ होती जा रही है। अब किस के पास सेल फ़ोन नहीं है? रोज़ कितनी नयी गाड़ियाँ सड़कों पर आ रही हैं। दिन-ब-दिन दिल्ली का नक़्शा बदलता जा रहा है। अब दिल्ली का शहर पहचाना भी नहीं जाता।

दीपक – हाँ, अब लगने लगा है कि बदलाव का चक्कर चलता ही रहेगा। अब मेट्रो भी शुरू हो गयी है। लोगों के पास बहुत दौलत हो गयी है, फिर भी लोग पैसों के पीछे दौड़ते रहते हैं। और अब दुकानों में कितनी चीज़ें मिलने लगी हैं!

कविता – कुछ लोगों के पास बहुत पैसे हो गये हैं, सभी लोगों के पास नहीं। और सब चीज़ों के दाम बढ़ते ही जा रहे हैं।

दीपक – यह तो सच है। पर क्या किया जाये? कुछ लोगों की ज़िंदगी अच्छी होती जा रही है और कुछ का जीवन और भी मुश्किल होता जा रहा है।

कविता – अगर यह कहा जाये कि अब यहाँ कुछ चीज़ें अच्छी हो गयी हैं और कुछ बुरी हो गयी हैं तो ग़लत नहीं होगा।

दीपक – लेकिन कुल मिलाकर मैं सोचता हूँ कि अब यहाँ तरक़्क़ी होती जा रही है।

कविता – शायद। दस साल बाद देखा जाएगा।

Translate the following questions based on the conversation and then take turns with a partner to ask and answer them. Listen to the online audio and answer these questions in Hindi in the pauses provided.

1. Where do Deepak and Kavita meet? ....

2. Was Kavita waiting for Deepak? ....

3. Does Deepak want to drink only tea? ....

4. Is life in Delhi continuing to change? (use imperfect part. + जाना) ....

5. Are many things now available in shops in Delhi? (*begun to be available*, use लगाना) ....

6. Does Kavita continually think about change? ....

7. Are the prices of things continuing to rise? (*increase*) ....

8. Does everyone (all people) have a lot of wealth now? (use हो जाना) ....

9. Does Deepak think that progress is continuing to take place in Delhi? ....

Glossary शब्दावली

The following words have appeared in the Activities that accompany Lesson 22. Most are common everyday words. Take a moment to study them along with the genders of the nouns.

अंधेरा dark

अकेला alone

अक्सर often

(x का) इंतज़ार करना to wait for x (*v.t.*)

कुल total (*m*)

कुल मिलाकर in total, overall

कौन-सा which (one)

खड़ा रहना to remain standing (*v.i.*)

खींचना to pull, draw (*v.t.*)

खो देना to lose (*v.t.*)

ग़लत wrong

चक्कर circle, revolution, rotation (*m*)

ज़िंदगी life (*f*)

तनख़्वाह salary (*f*)

तरक़्क़ी progress (*f*)

तस्वीर खींचना to take a picture (*v.t.*)

तुम्हारी मर्ज़ी your desire, whatever you want

तेज़ी से with speed, quickly

दिन-ब-दिन day after day

दो घंटे तक for two hours

दौड़ना to run (*v.i.*)

दौलत wealth (*f*)

नक़्शा map, shape (*m*)

पहचानना to recognize (*v.t.*)

बढ़ना to increase, grow (*v.i.*)

बदलना to change (*v.i.* + *v.t.*)

बिस्तर bedding, bed (*m*)

भविष्य future (*m*)

भारत यात्रा करना to travel to India (*v.t.*)

भाषण speech (*m*)

भिखारी beggar (*m*)

(x का) मन होना to feel like (x) (*v.i.*)

मिलाना to add, mix (*v.t.*)

यात्रा करना to travel, journey (*v.t.*)

x को y की याद आना x to miss y (*v.i.*)

रफ़्तार pace (*f*)

सारा entire, all

सोच में पड़ना to be deep in thought (*v.i.*)

हर every, all

LESSON **23** तेईसवाँ पाठ

Delhi Just Keeps Growing

ACTIVITY 23.1

Complete the following sentences and then translate the full sentence into fluid English. Then listen to them on the online audio, repeating them in the pauses provided.

1. _____ वह मुझे बहुत पसंद है।
   Which shirt you are wearing*

   _____

   * *Have worn* (use the coloring verb पहन रखना)

2. _____ मैं भी वहीं जाऊँगी।
   Wherever you may go

   _____

3. _____ वे आपको दे देंगे।
   Whatever you may want

   _____

4. _____ वे सब साल के अंत में भारत गये।
   Which students studied Hindi

   _____

5. तभी आप का काम हो पाएगा _____
   when you may study hard.*

   _____

   * *hard* = मन लगाकर (*having applied the heart/mind*)

6. _____ उतना ही करो।
   As much work *as* you may be able to do

   _____

ACTIVITY 23.2

Translate these sentences. Then listen to them on the online audio, repeating them in the pauses provided.

1. जब तक माँ अमरीका में काम करती रहीं तब तक हम बच्चे उनके साथ ही रहते थे।

2. जब तक यह चिट्ठी नहीं भेजी जाएगी तब तक उनको कैसे पता चलेगा कि हमारी शादी होनेवाली है?

3. जब तक आप गाड़ी चलाने का अभ्यास न करें तब तक आप अच्छी तरह कैसे सीखेंगे?

4. तब तक यह काम ख़त्म नहीं होगा जब तक तुम मेरी मदद नहीं करोगे।

5. जब तक मैं न आऊँ यहीं बैठे रहना।

6. Continue working until I say. (*until I may not say, until then continue doing work*)

7. They will have already gone by the time this happens. (*by when this happens, by then they will have already gone*) (use जा चुकना)

8. By the time I was able to finish my work he had no time for me. (*by when my work was finished, by then near him for me some time didn't remain*)

9. The snow will have melted on the mountains by the time you go there. (*by when you will go in the mountain, by then the snow will have melted*)

10. I will not be able to go until this happens. (*as long as this may not happen, until then I will not be able to go*)

ACTIVITY 23.3

Conversation बातचीत

🎧 Read and translate this conversation into English and then listen to it on the online audio. Here Deepak tells Kavita about a book that he has lost.

स्थान : कोई कैफ़े, नई दिल्ली
पात्र : कविता, दीपक

कविता – दीपक, तुम्हें आने में इतनी देर क्यों हुई? मैं तो आधे घंटे से इंतज़ार कर रही हूँ। मेरी कॉफ़ी ठंडी हो चुकी है।

दीपक – माफ़ करो, कविता। मेरी एक किताब खो गयी थी। मैं उसी की तलाश कर रहा था।

कविता – कौन-सी किताब?

दीपक – जिस किताब के बारे में मैंने तुम्हें बताया था। मैंने तुम्हारे लिये ख़रीद रखी थी।

कविता – मेरे लिये? सचमुच? जिस किताब की जिल्द का रंग लाल था वह वाली? वह जो बॉलीवुड सिनेमा के बारे में थी?

दीपक – हाँ, वह वाली किताब। मैं उसे लाइब्रेरी में लेकर गया था। और अब वह कहीं नहीं मिल रही।

कविता – जहाँ तुम लाइब्रेरी में बैठे थे, क्या वहाँ कोई और बैठा था?

दीपक – नहीं। वह बहुत सुनसान जगह है।

कविता – जिस समय तुम लाइब्रेरी में गये उस समय तुम किसी और के साथ थे?

दीपक – नहीं। मैं अकेले गया था। तुम भी नहीं थीं।

कविता – जैसे तुमने अभी अपना सामान पकड़ा है वैसे ही लाइब्रेरी में भी पकड़ा था?

दीपक – हाँ, क्यों? जब तक किताब न मिले तब तक मुझे चैन नहीं मिलेगा।

कविता – दीपक, तुमने अपने बस्ते में देख लिया होगा, न?

दीपक – कविता, क्या मुझे बेवकूफ़ समझती हो? बस्ते में कहाँ होगी किताब?

कविता – जो भी हो, एक बार देख लेना। कौन जाने, शायद मिल भी जाये।

दीपक – ओफ़ो, किताब तो है बस्ते में। मैं बहुत शर्मिंदा हूँ।

कविता – कोई बात नहीं। मेरे साथ ऐसा बहुत होता है। चलो चाय पियो।

Translate the following questions based on the conversation and then take turns with a partner to ask and answer them. Listen to the online audio and answer these questions in Hindi in the pauses provided.

1. Why was Deepak late? (*why did delay happen to Deepak*)

2. Since when was Kavita waiting?

3. For whom had Deepak bought the book?

4. Where had Deepak taken the book?

5. Was anyone else sitting where Deepak sits in the library?

6. As long as he doesn't find the book, will Deepak receive peace?

7. Must Deepak have looked in his bag? (No)

8. Is the book in Deepak's bag?

9. Does Kavita think Deepak is a fool?

Glossary शब्दावली

The following words have appeared in the Activities that accompany Lesson 23. Most are common everyday words. Take a moment to study them along with the genders of the nouns.

अकेले alone
अच्छी तरह well
अभ्यास practice (*m*)
आधा half
कौन जाने who knows
खोना to lose (*v.i. + v.t.*)
घंटा hour (*m*)
चाहना to want (*v.t.*)
चिट्ठी letter (*f*)
चैन peace, rest (*m*)
जगह place (*f*)

जहाँ भी wherever
जिल्द cover (*f*)
जो भी whatever
(x को) देर होना (x) to be late (*v.i.*)
पकड़ना to grab (*v.t.*)
पहनना to wear (*v.t.*)
पहाड़ mountain (*m*)
पिघलना to melt (*v.i.*)
बर्फ़ snow (*f*)
बस्ता bag, satchel (*m*)
बेवकूफ़ idiot, foolish

भेजना to send (*v.t.*)
मन लगाकर having applied the
  heart/mind, with industry
माफ़ करना to forgive (*v.t.*)
रंग color (*m*)
शर्मिंदा embarrassed
शादी marriage, wedding (*f*)
सचमुच really
समझना to understand, consider (*v.i. + v.t.*)
समय time (*m*)
सुनसान empty, desolate

LESSON 24 चौबीसवाँ पाठ

I Am Quite Worried about the Exams

ACTIVITY 24.1

🎧 Translate the following sentences and then listen to them on the online audio, repeating them in the pauses provided.

1. एक औरत आती हुई दिखाई दे रही थी।

   ....

2. मैंने अपने सोते हुए भाई को उठाया।

   ....

3. बहते हुए पानी में मत तैरना।

   ....

4. बार-बार बदलते विचार कभी दृढ़ नहीं होते।

   ....

5. बोलती हुई लड़की को चुप कराओ।

   ....

6. The pen lying on the table is mine. (*on the table laid pen mine is*)

   ....

7. The picture on the wall is very beautiful. (*on the wall attached picture is very beautiful*)

   ....

8. Don't throw away the money you have received. (*received money don't waste*)

   ....

9. Please close the open door. (*opened door*)

   ....

10. Don't eat that half-eaten roti.

....

ACTIVITY 24.2

Complete the following sentences and then translate them. Then listen to them on the online audio, repeating them in the pauses provided.

1. एक बार ....-चलते दीपक ने अपनी जेब में हाथ डाला। (चलना)

....

2. कल विश्वविद्यालय ....-समय वह अपनी लिखी एक चिट्ठी कविता को देना चाहता था। (जाना)

....

3. पर कविता से ....-वक़्त उसे लगा कि चिट्ठी खो गयी होगी। (मिलना)

....

4. पर अभी जेब में हाथ .... ही उसने देखा कि चिट्ठी तो कोट की जेब में ही पड़ी थी। (डालना)

....

5. अब जब कविता मिलेगी तो उसे वह .... हुए यह चिट्ठी दे देगा। (हँसना)

....

6. अपनी किताबें .... हुए वह और उसकी नयी दोस्त पुस्तकालय से बाहर निकले। (सँभालना)

....

7. होरी को उपवास .... हुए कई दिन हो गए थे। (करना)

....

8. भूख .... ही मनपसंद खाना उसके सामने आ जाता था। (लगना)

....

9. दीपक को कविता की याद आने लगी जिसे कल वह .... हुए छोड़ आया था। (रोना)

....

10. बच्चों के _____ समय ही वह अपनी पढ़ाई पूरी कर पाती थी। (सोना)

11. आज भी जब खाना न मिला तो मन ही मन तरह-तरह के पकवानों का स्वाद _____ हुए वह सो गया। (लेना)

ACTIVITY 24.3

🎧 Translate the following sentences and then listen to them on the online audio, repeating them in the pauses provided.

1. How long have you been reading this book? (*how many days*)

2. He has been living in India for two years.

3. They had been talking on the phone for four hours. (to talk = बातचीत करना)

4. At that time we had been selling books for 22 years.

5. How long have you been learning Hindi? (*how many years*)

6. I have been learning Hindi for nine months.

7. उन्हें बातचीत किये हुए दो घंटे हो गये।

8. मुझे हिन्दी सीखे नौ महीने हुए हैं।

9. उसे हिन्दुस्तान गये दो साल हो गये।

10. आपको हिन्दी सीखे हुए कितने बरस हो गये?

11. उस समय हमें घर बेचे हुए कुछ ही दिन हुए थे।

12. तुम्हें वह पुस्तक पढ़े कितने दिन हुए हैं?

ACTIVITY 24.4

Conversation बातचीत

Read and translate this conversation into English and then listen to it on the online audio. Here Deepak tries to express his emotions to Kavita.

स्थान : दिल्ली विश्वविद्यालय, नई दिल्ली
पात्र : कविता, दीपक

दीपक – कविता, तुम्हें दिल्ली में रहते हुए कितने साल हो गये हैं?

कविता – मुझे यहाँ रहते हुए दो साल हो गये हैं। और तुम्हें?

दीपक – मुझे भी दो साल हो गये हैं। तुम्हारे जो भाई ऑस्ट्रेलिया में रहते हैं उनको भारत आये हुए कितने दिन हुए हैं?

कविता – उन्हें इधर आये छै महीने हो गये हैं। उनको पत्र लिखते-समय उनकी बहुत ही याद आती है।

दीपक – अच्छा, कल मेरे लाइब्रेरी में पढ़ते-समय तुम क्या कर रही थीं?

कविता – उस समय मैं कोई किताब लिये अपने दोस्त के घर जा रही होऊँगी। क्यों?

दीपक – लाइब्रेरी से बाहर आते ही मैंने तुम्हें देखा था और अपने मन में सोचा कि मुझे तुम्हें पुकारना चाहिये। लेकिन मैं रुक गया और फिर तुम किसी गली में घुसकर ग़ायब हो गयी थीं।

कविता – मैं कहती रहती हूँ कि तुमको संकोच होना नहीं चाहिये। तुम ऐसा जानते हुए भी कि मुझे तुम्हारे साथ अच्छा लगता है बहुत घबराए रहते हो।

दीपक – ऐसी बात नहीं है। तुमसे बिना बात किये मैं घर जाना नहीं चाहता था।

कविता – अगर मैं तुम्हारी जगह होती तो तुमसे मिले बिना मैं रह नहीं सकती। चलो अभी घर जाना चाहिये। पहुँचते-पहुँचते रात हो जाएगी।

दीपक – कविता! क्या तुम ...

कविता – क्या दीपक? तुम्हें क्या कहना है? कहते-कहते क्यों रुक गये? क्या बात है?

दीपक – कुछ नहीं। घर जाने से पहले क्या मेरे साथ कॉफ़ी पीने जाओगी?

कविता – ठीक है। लेकिन जल्दी क्योंकि मुझे रात को बाहर जाना है।

दीपक – (मन ही मन) क्या कैफ़े में मैं मन की बात बताने की हिम्मत जुटा पाऊँगा?

Translate the following questions based on the conversation and then take turns with a partner to ask and answer them. Listen to the online audio and answer these questions in Hindi in the pauses provided.

1. How long has Kavita been living in Delhi?

2. How long have you been living here?

3. How long has Deepak been living in Delhi?

4. How long has it been since Kavita's brother came to India?

5. How long is it since you have been to India?*

   * If you have never been to India, you can answer मैं हिन्दुस्तान कभी नहीं गया/गयी।

6. Where must Kavita have been going when Deepak was studying in the library?

7. Should Deepak have called out to Kavita?

8. Does Kavita have to go out tonight?

9. Do you have to go out tonight? (yes)

10. Should Deepak tell Kavita how he feels? (*the matter of his heart*)

Glossary शब्दावली

The following words have appeared in the Activities that accompany Lesson 24. Most are common everyday words. Take a moment to study them along with the genders of the nouns.

उठाना to raise, lift up, wake up (*v.t.*)

उपवास fast (not eating) (*m*)

x की जगह in place of x

x के बिना without x

खो जाना to become lost (*v.i.*)

गँवाना to waste, lose (*v.t.*)

गली lane, gully (*f*)

ग़ायब होना to disappear (*v.i.*)

घबराना to be nervous (*v.i.*)

घुसना to enter, penetrate (*v.i.*)

चुप कराना to shut up (someone) (*v.t.*)

जेब pocket (*f*)

डालना to put, place (*v.t.*)

तरह-तरह all manner

तैरना to swim (*v.i.*)

दृढ़ firm, solid

पकवान rich fried foods for festive occasions (*m pl*)

पुकारना to call (out) (*v.t.*)

बरस year (*m*)

मन heart, mind (*m*)

मन ही मन in the mind

मनपसंद favorite

रुकना to stop (*v.i.*)

संकोच hesitation, shyness, embarrassment (*m*)

संभालना to steady, maintain, to take care (of) (*v.t.*)

स्वाद taste (*m*)

हिम्मत जुटाना to summon courage (*v.t.*)

Answer Key

Lesson 1

Activity 1.3

1. What is a mango?
2. Is this a mango?
3. This is a yellow mango.
4. What is salt?
5. Is this salt?
6. This is less salt.
7. What is that story?
8. Is that a story?
9. That is a story.
10. What is a lotus?
11. Is that a red lotus?
12. Is that lotus red?

Activity 1.4

1. क्या यह पक्का मकान है?
2. यह पक्का मकान है।
3. यह क्या है?
4. वह कापी है।
5. क्या यह पहला महीना है?
6. वह क्या है?
7. यह लाल क़लम है।
8. क्या वह क़लम लाल है?
9. यह क़लम लाल है।
10. यह पानी नीला है।
11. क्या यह पान है?
12. वह पान है।
13. पान क्या है?
14. क्या यह कम काम है?

Lesson 2

Activity 2.2

1. This is our room.
2. Where is your room?
3. Is that sitar cheap?
4. Yes, this sitar is cheap.
5. I have a question.
6. What is your question?
7. What is the price of one pen?
8. The price of one pen is one *paisa*.
9. Is this a/the new market?
10. No, this is the red market.

Activity 2.3

1. मेरा नाम दीपक है।
2. आपका नाम क्या है?
3. मेरा नाम कविता है।
4. किताब का दाम क्या है?
5. आपकी बहन कहाँ है?
6. क्या उसका मकान नया है?
7. जी हाँ, उसका मकान नया है।
8. क्या यह मेरी क़मीज़ है?
9. जी नहीं, वह आपकी बहन की क़मीज़ है।
10. क्या यह आदमी की आवाज़ है?
11. आपका पता क्या है?
12. जी नहीं, मेरी बहन यहाँ नहीं है।

Activity 2.4

1. जी नहीं, वह उसकी किताब है।
2. जी हाँ, ये मेरे माँ-बाप हैं।
3. जी नहीं, यह आपकी क़मीज़ है।
4. जी हाँ, यह उनका कमरा है।
5. जी नहीं, वे आपके सितार नहीं हैं।
6. जी हाँ, यह उनका सामान है।
7. जी नहीं, यह उनकी दवा है।

Activity 2.5: Conversation

Deepak : Hello, *ji*. Are you Kavita's mother?

Sunita : Yes. What is your name?

Deepak : *Ji*, my name is Deepak.

Sunita : Is your house here?

Deepak : No, our house is not here. My mother and father are in Allahabad. But one of my uncles is here.

Sunita : Where is your uncle's house?

Deepak : It is in front.

Kavita : Deepak, hello. Mom, this is Deepak.

Deepak : Hello Kavita.

Kavita : Deepak, where is your sister?

Deepak : These days she is in Allahabad. Kavita, is this your book?

Kavita : Yes, this is my book.

Deepak : What is its price?

Kavita : Its price is thirty rupees.

Deepak : Is it a storybook (story)?

Kavita : Yes, this is a storybook (story).

1. कविता की माँ का नाम क्या है? कविता की माँ का नाम सुनीता है।
2. आपका नाम क्या है? मेरा नाम ... है। (Write your name in Roman.)
3. दीपक के माँ-बाप कहाँ हैं? दीपक के माँ-बाप इलाहाबाद में हैं।
4. क्या दीपक का मकान इलाहाबाद में है? जी हाँ, दीपक का मकान इलाहाबाद में है।
5. आजकल दीपक की बहन कहाँ है? आजकल दीपक की बहन इलाहाबाद में है।
6. कविता की किताब का दाम क्या है? कविता की किताब का दाम तीस रुपये है।

Lesson 3

Activity 3.2

1. आज का मौसम कैसा है? How is today's weather?
2. आज का मौसम ख़राब है। Today's weather is bad.
3. क्या यह सस्ती दवा है? Is this (a) cheap medicine?
4. जी हाँ, यह दवा सस्ती है। Yes, this medicine is cheap.
5. क्या ये आपके पीले आम हैं? Are these your yellow mangoes?
6. जी हाँ, ये मेरे पीले आम हैं। Yes, these are my yellow mangoes.
7. बाहर कितने आदमी खड़े हैं? How many men are standing outside?
8. बाहर पाँच आदमी खड़े हैं। There are five men standing outside.
9. क्या आपकी किताब आसान है? Is your book easy?
10. जी हाँ, मेरी किताब आसान है। Yes, my book is easy.
11. क्या वह ताज़ा तरकारी है? Is that a fresh vegetable?
12. जी नहीं, वह बासी तरकारी है। No, that is a stale (rotten) vegetable.
13. क्या आप ख़ाली हैं? Are you free (available)?
14. जी नहीं, मैं ख़ाली नहीं हूँ। No, I am not free.
15. यह सारी दीवार ख़राब है क्या? Is this entire wall bad?
16. जी हाँ, वह ख़राब है। Yes, it is bad.
17. वह लड़की कैसी है? How is that girl?
18. वह लड़की बहुत ख़ूबसूरत है। That girl is very beautiful.

Activity 3.3

1. यह लड़का बहुत बड़ा है।
2. वह बहुत बड़ी लड़की है।
3. आज की तारीख़ क्या है?
4. आज दो तारीख़ है।
5. वहाँ तीन आदमी खड़े हैं।
6. वहाँ चार ताज़ा आलू हैं।
7. दवा की बोतल नीली है।
8. उसकी साड़ी लाल है।

Activity 3.4: Conversation

Kavita : Hello Deepak. How are you?

Deepak : Hello Kavita. I am in fine spirits. How are you (how is your state)?

Kavita : Fine. How bad is the weather today!

Deepak : No, today's weather isn't so bad.

Kavita : Deepak, today's weather is really bad.

Deepak : What is the date today, Kavita *ji*?

Kavita : Today is the second.

Deepak : Are you free?

Kavita : Yes Deepak, I am free. What is the task?

Deepak : (I have) a bit of Hindi work.

Kavita : So where is your Hindi book?

Deepak : It is on the big table.

Kavita : There is a blue medicine bottle on the table, not a book.

Deepak : Not there, over here.

Kavita : Oh, yes. This is your book.

1. आज दीपक कैसा है? आज दीपक मज़े में है।
2. क्या कविता मज़े में है? जी हाँ, कविता मज़े में है। जी नहीं, कविता मज़े में नहीं है।
3. आज आपका क्या हाल है? आज मैं मज़े में हूँ।
4. आज क्या आप ख़ाली हैं? जी हाँ, आज मैं ख़ाली हूँ। जी नहीं, आज मैं ख़ाली नहीं हूँ।
5. क्या आज का मौसम ख़राब है? जी हाँ, आज का मौसम ख़राब है। जी नहीं, आज का मौसम ख़राब नहीं है।
6. बड़ी मेज़ पर क्या है? बड़ी मेज़ पर दवा की नीली बोतल है। बड़ी मेज़ पर एक किताब है। बड़ी मेज़ पर एक नीली बोतल और एक किताब हैं।
7. क्या बड़ी मेज़ पर दवा की एक नीली बोतल है? जी हाँ, बड़ी मेज़ पर दवा की एक नीली बोतल है।

Lesson 4

Activity 4.2

1. नमस्ते जी, आप कैसे हैं? Hello *ji*, how are you (*m*)?
2. नमस्कार जी, आप कैसी हैं? Hello *ji*, how are you (*f*)?
3. आप का नाम क्या है? What is your name?
4. मेरा नाम दीपक है। My name is Deepak.
5. और तू कौन है? And who are you?
6. जी, मैं कविता हूँ। *Ji*, I am Kavita.
7. दीपक, आजकल तुम्हारी बहन कहाँ है? Where is your sister these days, Deepak?
8. क्या तुम आजकल इलाहाबाद में हो? Are you in Allahabad these days?
9. इनके दोस्त यहाँ नहीं हैं। Their/His/Her friends are not here.
10. किसका दोस्त वहाँ है? Whose friend is there?
11. यहाँ कितने मकान हैं? How many houses are here?

12. अब किसकी बारी <u>है</u>? Whose turn is (it) now?

13. उस की बारी <u>है</u>। (It) is his/her turn.

Activity 4.3

1. मेरी नीली क़मीज़ मेज़ पर है।

2. तुम्हारी किताब की दुकान बहुत बड़ी है।

3. मेज़ पर कितने पुराने अख़बार हैं?

4. मेज़ पर पाँच पुराने अख़बार हैं।

5. हमारी चाय ताज़ा है।

6. क्या आपकी चाय में काफ़ी चीनी है?

7. कल का दूध ख़राब है।

8. ये किसके ख़ूबसूरत फूल हैं?

9. आपकी घड़ी काफ़ी नयी है।

10. किसी की काँच की चूड़ी मेज़ पर है।

Activity 4.4: Conversation

Juhi : Hello. What's your name?

Deepak : *Ji*, I am Deepak. And who are you?

Juhi : I am Juhi. Where is Kavita?

Deepak : Kavita is outside.

Juhi : Right. Who is standing over there?

Deepak : That is my uncle.

Juhi : What is his name?

Deepak : His name is Kripa Lal. Where is Kavita's family?

Juhi : Her mother is standing outside. Hey Kavita, come here. Where's your father?

Kavita : Hi Juhi. My father is standing outside. Oh Deepak, how are you?

Deepak : Good thanks. How are you?

Kavita : My throat is a little sore today. Juhi, your house is very beautiful. But there are a lot of people here today.

Juhi : Yes, they are all father's friends.

Deepak : Kavita, these flowers are for you.

Kavita : These are very beautiful.

Juhi : What's this?

Deepak : It's nothing, really.

1. कविता की दोस्त का नाम क्या है? कविता की दोस्त का नाम जुही है।

2. कविता की माँ कहाँ खड़ी है? कविता की माँ बाहर खड़ी है।

3. क्या जुही का मकान बहुत ख़ूबसूरत है? जी हाँ, जुही का मकान बहुत ख़ूबसूरत है।

4. क्या आज कविता का गला ख़राब है? जी हाँ, आज कविता का गला ख़राब है।

5. फूल किसके लिये हैं? फूल कविता के लिये हैं।

6. क्या जुही कविता की दोस्त है? जी हाँ, जुही कविता की दोस्त है।

Lesson 5

Activity 5.2

1. उसकी किताब वहाँ थी। His/Her book was (over) there.

2. कल आप कहाँ थीं? (f) Where were you (f) yesterday?

3. आपके पिता जी घर में थे। You father was at home.

4. वह यहाँ नहीं था। (m) He was not (over) there.

5. तुम स्कूल में क्यों नहीं थीं? (f) Why were you (f) not at school?

6. कल मैं कॉलेज में था। (m) Yesterday I (m) was in college.

7. वह बिलकुल बेवफ़ा था। (m) He was completely unfaithful.

8. कल सोमवार था। Yesterday was Monday.

9. इनके दोस्त यहाँ नहीं थे। Their/His/Her friend(s) was (were) not here.

10. कल मौसम कैसा था? How was the weather yesterday?

11. यहाँ कितने खूबसूरत मकान थे? How many beautiful houses were here?

12. क़लम का दाम क्या था? What was the price of the pen?

Activity 5.3

1. यह दीवार कितनी ऊँची है? यह दीवार बहुत ऊँची है।

2. आज तुम कैसे हो? आज मैं ठीक हूँ।

3. यहाँ कितने अख़बार थे? यहाँ कई अख़बार थे।

4. वह कैसा अख़बार है? वह अख़बार अच्छा है।

5. वह अख़बार कैसा है? वह बहुत अच्छा नहीं है।

6. वह कैसी दुकान थी? वह बहुत बड़ी दुकान थी।

7. दुनिया में कितने लोग हैं? क्या बेकार का सवाल है।

8. वह आदमी कैसा था? वह आदमी बेवफ़ा था।

9. वे फूल कितने खूबसूरत थे? हाँ, बहुत।

10. वह कैसा काम था? वह अच्छा काम था।

Activity 5.4: Conversation

Deepak : Hello Kavita. How are you?

Kavita : Hi Deepak. I am absolutely fine. How are you (how is your state)?

Deepak : Fine. I am fine. Where were you yesterday, Kavita?

Kavita : Yesterday I was at home. I was sick. What a great day it is today!

Deepak : Yes, it is very good. Oh, how is this book?

Kavita : It is not that good, but it is okay.

Deepak : Where are your friends today?

Kavita : They are not at college today.

Deepak : How many classes do you have today?

Kavita : I have four classes today.

Deepak : How many people are standing in the bookstore over there?

Kavita : There are three people. How is that shop?

Deepak : It is good.

Kavita : Okay, Deepak. Bye.

Deepak : Bye Kavita.

1. क्या आज कविता बिल्कुल ठीक है? जी हाँ, आज कविता बिल्कुल ठीक है।

2. कल कविता कहाँ थी? कल कविता घर में थी।

3. कल क्या कविता बीमार थी? जी हाँ, कल कविता बीमार थी।

4. कल क्या आप बीमार थे/थीं? जी हाँ, कल मैं बीमार था/थी। जी नहीं, कल मैं बीमार नहीं था/थी।

5. कल क्या आपके भाई बीमार थे? कल क्या आपकी बहन बीमार थीं?

   Can also be: कल क्या आपका भाई बीमार था? and कल क्या आपकी बहन बीमार थी?

   जी हाँ, कल मेरे भाई बीमार थे। जी हाँ, कल मेरी बहन बीमार थीं।

6. क्या आज का मौसम अच्छा है? जी हाँ, आज का मौसम अच्छा है। जी नहीं, आज का मौसम अच्छा नहीं है।

7. दुकान में कितने लोग खड़े हैं? दुकान में तीन लोग खड़े हैं।

8. दुकान कैसी है? दुकान तो अच्छी है।

Lesson 6

Activity 6.2

1. अक्खड़ headstrong, contemptuous, rude

2. संस्कृत cultured, refined; Sanskrit (language) (*f*)

3. दुष्टात्मा wicked, vicious, vile

4. ऐंद्रिय sensual, pertaining to the senses

5. ऐतिह्य tradition (*m*)

6. मुद्रा a seal, stamp, money, demeanor, mien, pose, posture (*f*)

7. राष्ट्र nation (*m*)

8. फ़र्श floor (of a room), flooring (*m*)

9. व्यक्ति individual, person, subject (*m*)

10. उन्नति progress, rise; promotion, improvement (*f*)

11. शून्य empty, void; vacant; hollow, desolate

12. ऐश्वर्य opulence; prosperity, glory and grandeur (*m*)

13. अंतर्मुखी introverted

14. विज्ञान science (*m*)

15. अक्षर any letter of the alphabet, character; syllable (*m*)

16. पवित्र holy, sacred; pure

Activity 6.3

1. What (which) day is today?

2. Today is Wednesday.

3. What day was yesterday?

4. Yesterday was Tuesday.

5. Where were you (*f*) yesterday morning?

6. I (*f*) was not here yesterday morning.

7. Why were you (*m*) not here last night?

8. Last night I (*m*) was right here.

9. When did this happen (it is a matter of when)?

10. This happened on Thursday (it was Thursday's matter).

Activity 6.4

1. आज शनिवार है।

2. कल शुक्रवार था।

3. कल रविवार है।

4. उसके चार भाई हैं।

5. उसकी एक बहन है।

6. यह मार्च का महीना है।

Activity 6.5: Conversation

Deepak : Hey Kavita. What brings you here (how are you here)? Where were you last night?

Kavita : I was just at home. Why?

Deepak : No reason. Oh, is this my Hindi book? Where was it?

Kavita : It was on my table.

Deepak : Oh, thanks. Come inside. Tea or coffee?

Kavita : Nothing right now, thanks. Deepak, how many brothers and sisters do you have?

Deepak : We are three brothers and sisters. I have an older brother and a younger sister.

Kavita : Where are they all now?

Deepak : My sister is in Allahabad. And my brother is right here. You have one brother, right?

Kavita : Yes, but he is in Australia these days.

Deepak : How long has he been in Australia?

Kavita : He has been in Australia for two years.

1. कल रात कविता कहाँ थी? कल रात कविता घर में ही थी।

2. कल रात क्या कविता घर में ही थी? जी हाँ, कल रात कविता घर में ही थी।

3. दीपक की किताब कहाँ थी? दीपक की किताब कविता की मेज़ पर थी।

4. दीपक के कितने भाई हैं? दीपक का एक भाई है।

5. दीपक का भाई बड़ा है, या छोटा? दीपक का भाई बड़ा है।

6. आपके कितने भाई हैं? मेरा एक भाई है। मेरे दो भाई हैं। मेरा कोई भाई नहीं है।

7. क्या आपकी बहन है? जी हाँ, मेरी एक बहन है। जी हाँ, मेरी दो बहनें हैं।* जी नहीं, मेरी कोई बहन नहीं है।

   * Note that बहनें is the plural form of बहन. For a full description of feminine nouns and their declension, see Textbook p. 59.

8. क्या कविता का भाई ऑस्ट्रेलिया में है?* जी हाँ, कविता का भाई ऑस्ट्रेलिया में है।

   * Note that, for respect, this can also be expressed employing plural forms. (क्या कविता के भाई ऑस्ट्रेलिया में हैं?)

9. वह वहाँ कब से है? वह वहाँ दो साल से है।

Lesson 7

Activity 7.1

दाम a/the price	दाम में in a/the price	दाम (the) prices	दामों में in (the) prices
पेड़ a/the tree	पेड़ में in a/the tree	पेड़ (the) trees	पेड़ों में in (the) trees
पिता (a/the) father	पिता में in a/the father	पिता (the) fathers	पिताओं में in (the) fathers
लड़का a/the boy	लड़के में in a/the boy	लड़के (the) boys	लड़कों में in (the) boys
कमरा a/the room	कमरे में in a/the room	कमरे (the) rooms	कमरों में in (the) rooms
आदमी a/the man	आदमी में in a/the man	आदमी (the) men	आदमियों में in (the) men
फल a/the fruit	फल में in a/the fruit	फल (the) fruits	फलों में in (the) fruits
मंत्री a/the minister	मंत्री में in a/the minister	मंत्री (the) ministers	मंत्रियों में in (the) ministers
लिफ़ाफ़ा an/the envelope	लिफ़ाफ़े में in an/the envelope	लिफ़ाफ़े (the) envelopes	लिफ़ाफ़ों में in (the) envelopes
पति a/the husband	पति में in a/the husband	पति (the) husbands	पतियों में in (the) husbands
संवाददाता a/the correspondent	संवाददाता में in a/the correspondent	संवाददाता (the) correspondents	संवाददाताओं में in (the) correspondents
कुआँ a/the well (water)	कुएँ में in a/the well	कुएँ (the) wells	कुओं में in (the) wells
भालू a/the bear	भालू में in a/the bear	भालू (the) bears	भालुओं में in (the) bears
कीड़ा an/the insect	कीड़े में in an/the insect	कीड़े (the) insects	कीड़ों में in (the) insects
राजा a/the king	राजा में in a/the king	राजा (the) kings	राजाओं में in (the) kings

Activity 7.2

1. आप का पता क्या है? What is your address?
2. उन सितारों का दाम क्या है? What is the price of those sitars?
3. वहाँ कितने आदमी खड़े हैं? How many men are standing over there?
4. एक सेब का दाम दस रुपये है। The price of one apple is ten rupees.
5. इस कमरे में कौन है? Who is in this room?
6. पान किसको चाहिये? Who wants *pān*?
7. उन आदमियों में से कौन अच्छा है? Who is good from among those men?
8. मेरे गले में दर्द है। I have a pain in my throat.
9. तेरे कितने मामा हैं? How many uncles do you have?
10. आलू में कीड़े हैं। There are worms in the potato.

Activity 7.3

1. यह कमरा काफ़ी बड़ा है।
2. बड़े कमरे के साथ क्या गुसलख़ाना था?
3. कितने कमरे ख़ाली हैं?
4. कुछ कमरों में चार पलंग थे।
5. इस कमरे का किराया क्या है?
6. मेरे पिता जी के सिर में दर्द है।
7. इन दो होटलों के मालिक कौन हैं?
8. उन दो मकानों में तीन आदमी थे।
9. धोबी कहाँ हैं?
10. तुम्हारे कितने भाई हैं?

Activity 7.4

1. आपको क्या चाहिये? What do you want/need?
2. मुझे/मुझको कुछ नहीं चाहिये। I want/need nothing.
3. कल उन्हें/उनको क्या चाहिये था? What did they/he/she want/need yesterday?
4. कल इसे/इसको दो कमरे चाहिये थे। Yesterday he/she wanted/needed two rooms.
5. अगले हफ़्ते किसे/किसको काम चाहिये? Next week who wants/needs work?
6. अगले हफ़्ते हमें/हमको काम चाहिये। Next week we/I want/need work.
7. किसी को धन नहीं चाहिये। No one wants/needs wealth.
8. इन्हें/इनको पाँच संतरे चाहिये। He/She/They want(s)/need(s) five oranges.
9. क्या तुम्हें/तुमको उस कमरे में पलंग चाहिये? Do you want/need a bed in that room?
10. उसे/उसको बढ़िया कपड़े चाहिये। He/She wants/needs excellent clothes.

Activity 7.5: Conversation

Kavita : Hello *ji*. How are you?
Owner : I am absolutely fine. How are you?
Kavita : Okay, I am well. Sir, I need a room.
Owner : For whom do you need the room?
Kavita : The room is not actually for me. One of my father's friends needs the room.
Owner : Is your father's friend Indian?
Kavita : No, he is not from India. He is American. He needs a room next week.
Owner : Okay, for how many days does he need the room?
Kavita : He needs the room for five days. Does every room have a bathroom?
Owner : Yes, there are bathrooms with both the single and double rooms.
Kavita : Good. And there is hot water in the hotel as well, isn't there?
Owner : Yes, yes, certainly.
Kavita : So what is the rate of a single room?

Owner : The rate of a single room is one thousand five hundred rupees per day, and of a double room two thousand five hundred rupees per day.

Kavita : Okay, how many other hotels are there nearby?

Owner : There are many hotels in the city. Why?

Kavita : No reason. Okay, where is the room?

Owner : Yes, yes, come this way.

1. कविता को क्या चाहिये? कविता को एक कमरा चाहिए।

2. आपको क्या चाहिये? मुझे चाय चाहिए। (पैसे, शांति, कॉफ़ी)

3. कविता को किस के लिये एक कमरा चाहिये? कविता को पिता जी के एक दोस्त के लिये एक कमरा चाहिये।

4. क्या कविता के पिता जी का दोस्त भारत का है? जी नहीं, कविता के पिता जी का दोस्त भारत का नहीं है।

5. क्या आप भारत के/की हैं? जी हाँ, मैं भारत का/की हूँ। जी नहीं, मैं भारत का/की नहीं हूँ।

6. क्या आपके माता-पिता भारत के हैं? जी हाँ, वे भारत के हैं। जी नहीं, वे भारत के नहीं हैं, वे ... के हैं।

7. कविता के पिता जी के दोस्त को कमरा कब चाहिये? कविता के पिता जी के दोस्त को कमरा अगले हफ़्ते चाहिये।

8. उसे/उसको कितने दिन के लिए कमरा चाहिए? उसे/उसको पाँच दिन के लिए कमरा चाहिए।

9. सिंगल कमरे का किराया क्या है? सिंगल कमरे का किराया डेढ़ हज़ार रुपये रोज़ है।

10. क्या शहर में बहुत होटल हैं? जी हाँ, शहर में बहुत होटल हैं।

Lesson 8

Activity 8.1

भाषा	भाषा के लिये	भाषाएँ	भाषाओं के लिये
a/the language	for a/the language	(the) languages	for (the) languages
वस्तु	वस्तु के लिए	वस्तुएँ	वस्तुओं के लिए
a/the thing	for a/the thing	(the) things	for (the) things
चिड़िया	चिड़िया के लिए	चिड़ियाँ	चिड़ियों के लिए
a/the bird	for a/the bird	(the) birds	for (the) birds
रस्सी	रस्सी के लिये	रस्सियाँ	रस्सियों के लिये
a/the rope	for a/the rope	(the) ropes	for (the) ropes
छत	छत के लिए	छतें	छतों के लिए
a/the roof	for a/the roof	(the) roofs	for (the) roofs
आज्ञा	आज्ञा के लिये	आज्ञाएँ	आज्ञाओं के लिए
an/the order	for an/the order	(the) orders	for (the) orders
गुड़िया	गुड़िया के लिए	गुड़ियाँ	गुड़ियों के लिये
a/the doll	for a/the doll	(the) doll	for (the) dolls
पत्नी	पत्नी के लिये	पत्नियाँ	पत्नियों के लिए
a/the wife	for a/the wife	(the) wives	for (the) wives
कविता	कविता के लिए	कविताएँ	कविताओं के लिये
a/the poem	for a/the poem	(the) poems	for (the) poems

ख़बर	ख़बर के लिए	ख़बरें	ख़बरों के लिए
a/the news	for a/the news	(the) news	for (the) news

छुट्टी	छुट्टी के लिये	छुट्टियाँ	छुट्टियों के लिये
a/the holiday	for a/the holiday	(the) holidays	for (the) holidays

Activity 8.2

1. इन लड़कियों की माँ वहाँ खड़ी थीं। The mother of these girls was standing over there.
2. आप की कितनी बहनें हैं? How many sisters do you have?
3. क्या ये उन बहनों के कपड़े हैं? Are these the clothes of those sisters?
4. इस बाज़ार में कितनी दुकानें थीं? How many shops were in this market?
5. उस बाज़ार की दुकानों में अच्छा सामान नहीं है। There is no good merchandise in the shops in that market.
6. इस साड़ी का कपड़ा क्या है? What is the material of this sari?
7. इन साड़ियों में कुछ छेद हैं। There are some holes in these saris.
8. हिन्दुस्तान में कितनी भाषाएँ हैं? How many languages are there in India?
9. क्या आपके मन में कोई इच्छा है? Is there any desire in your heart?
10. जी हाँ, मेरे मन में बहुत इच्छाएँ हैं। Yes, there are many desires in my heart.

Activity 8.3

Give me a pen. Sell him/her a picture. Take this book. तू

Don't give him/her dolls. Sell me ropes. Don't take that stick. तुम

Please give us pens. Please do not sell them/him/her tables. Please take a samosa. आप

Please give them/him/her watches. Please sell medicine to him/her. Please take these bottles. आप

Give someone sweets. Sell us good things. Don't take his/her gift. तू/तुम

Activity 8.4

1. यह मेरी हिन्दी की किताब है।
2. इस किताब में बीस पन्ने हैं।
3. मेज़ पर चार किताबें हैं।
4. इन चार किताबों में कुछ सुन्दर तस्वीरें हैं।
5. उस आदमी की पत्नी आँगन में खड़ी थी।
6. उन आदमियों की पत्नियाँ आँगन में खड़ी थीं।
7. उस आदमी की पत्नी को यह किताब दीजिये (दो)।
8. उन आदमियों की पत्नियों को ये किताबें दीजिये (दो)।
9. उस किताब में एक सुन्दर कविता है।
10. इस किताब में कुछ सुन्दर कविताएँ हैं।

Activity 8.5: Conversation

Sunita : Kavita, you order for everyone.
Kavita : Okay, mom. Deepak, what do you want?
Deepak : I want tea. Kavita, say, what do you want?
Kavita : I just want coffee.
Sunita : Kavita, have something to eat.
Kavita : No, mom, I don't want anything.
Deepak : *Ji*, please tell (us). What would you like?
Sunita : I just want tea. Okay Kavita?
Kavita : Absolutely. Brother-Sir! Are you ready? Take our order.
Waiter : Yes, please tell (me).
Deepak : Bring us two coffees and one tea.
Kavita : Deepak, don't you speak. Brother-Sir, bring two teas and one coffee.
Sunita : Deepak, have something to eat as well. Don't be formal.

Kavita   : Mom, don't force (him).
Deepak   : Okay, bring two samosas for me.
Kavita   : So, how many things do we want? Two teas, one coffee and two samosas. Does anyone want anything else? Mom, (do) you?
Sunita   : No, (my) daughter. This much is enough.
Kavita   : Bring it hot. Don't bring anything cold. The samosas are fresh, aren't they?
Waiter   : *Ji* absolutely.

1. दीपक को क्या चाहिये? दीपक को चाय और दो समोसे चाहिये।
2. क्या कविता को सिर्फ़ चाय चाहिए? जी हाँ, कविता को सिर्फ़ चाय चाहिए।
3. सब लोगों को क्या-क्या चाहिये? कविता की माँ को सिर्फ़ चाय चाहिये। कविता को कॉफ़ी चाहिए और दीपक को चाय और दो समोसे चाहिये।
4. दीपक को कितने समोसे चाहिए? दीपक को दो समोसे चाहिए।
5. क्या समोसे ताज़े (ताज़ा) हैं? जी हाँ, समोसे ताज़े (ताज़ा) हैं।
6. क्या आपको अभी चाय चाहिये? जी हाँ, मुझे अभी चाय चाहिये। जी नहीं, मुझे अभी चाय नहीं चाहिये।

Lesson 9

Activity 9.1

1. मैं (m) हिन्दी पढ़ता हूँ। I study Hindi.
2. हम (f) रोज़ अख़बार पढ़ती हैं। We (f) read the newspaper every day.
3. वह (m) पत्र लिखता है। He writes a letter.
4. वे (f) बहुत काम नहीं करतीं। They (f) don't do much work.
5. तुम (f) वहाँ क्यों नहीं जातीं? Why don't you (f) go there?
6. मैं (f) कभी-कभी फ़िल्में देखती हूँ। I (f) occasionally watch films.
7. यह (m) बहुत शराब पीता है। He drinks a lot of alcohol.
8. आप (m) स्कूल कब पहुँचते हैं? When do you (m) arrive at school?
9. तू (m) अमरीका में रहता है। You (m) live in America.
10. हम (m) कुछ पैसा नहीं देते। We (m) do not give any money.
11. आप (f) खाना कब खाती हैं? When do you (m) eat food?
12. वह (f) किस कमरे में सोती है? In which room does she sleep?
13. तुम (m) जल्दी क्यों उठते हो? Why do you (m) get up early?
14. तू (m) फूल क्यों तोड़ता है? Why do you (m) pluck/break flowers?
15. यह (m) क्यों नहीं सोचता? Why does he not think?
16. ये (f) कुछ नहीं कहतीं। She/they (f) say(s) nothing.
17. वे (m) बहुत मेहनत करते हैं। He/they work(s) hard.
18. ये (m) हमेशा मेरी गाड़ी लेते हैं। He/they always take(s) my car.

Activity 9.2

1. मैं किताबें बेचता हूँ।
2. मैं लोगों को किताबें बेचती हूँ।
3. वे जलेबियाँ खाती हैं।
4. वह उन दुकानदारों को जानता है।
5. तुम मुझे/मुझको हिन्दी सिखाती हो। (आप सिखाती हैं)
6. हम अंग्रेज़ी पढ़ते हैं।
7. वह लड़के को अच्छे कपड़े पहनाती है।
8. आप मुझे/मुझको चाय पिलाते हैं। (तुम पिलाते हो)
9. मैं उसे रोज़ पढ़ती हूँ।
10. वे तुम्हारे भाइयों को जानते हैं। (आपके)

Activity 9.3

1. सोमवार को मेरे घर मत आइये।

2. क्या आप मंगलवार को कॉलेज जाते हैं? (मंगल को)

3. बुधवार को मैं हिन्दी पढ़ता हूँ। (बुध को)

4. गुरुवार को मैं छात्रों को हिन्दी सिखाती हूँ। (गुरु को)

5. शुक्रवार को हमारी छुट्टी है। (शुक्र को)

6. शनिवार को हम मेरे दोस्त के घर जाते हैं।

7. इतवार को हम कुछ नहीं करते।

8. Phone me on the first.

9. Please come to my place on the second. (तुम)

10. Don't go to university on the third. (आप)

11. I pay the rent for (my) apartment every (month on the) 4th.

12. His/her birthday was on the fifth.

Activity 9.4

1. Her name is Kavita.

2. The name of that girl is Kavita.

3. The price of this is two rupees.

4. The price of a *jalebi* is two rupees.

5. This is his/her new house.

6. The price of this new house is a lot.

7. The name of that older brother is Deepak.

8. His/her older brother's name is Deepak.

9. This good friend's book is over there.

10. His/her good friend's book is on the table.

11. There is a *jalebi* in that *jalebi* shop.

12. There are *jalebis* in his/her *jalebi* shop.

13. There is a girl near that small room.

14. There is a girl near his/her small room.

Activity 9.5: Conversation

Kavita : Hello, I am Deepak's friend Kavita. What's your name?

Vrinda : My name is Vrinda. I am Deepak's sister.

Kavita : Good, is Deepak at home?

Vrinda : Yes, come inside. Sit. What do you do?

Kavita : I study in college, with Deepak. And you?

Vrinda : I also study, but in Allabahad. How many brothers and sisters do you have?

Kavita : I have one brother. He is in Australia these days.

Vrinda : What does he do?

Kavita : He doesn't work. He also studies.

Vrinda : What do you study? Medicine?

Kavita : Yes, it is my intention to become a doctor.

Vrinda : Good. I will call Deepak. Oh Hiralal! Make some tea for Kavita.

Kavita : No Vrinda, I don't need tea at the moment (right now). Please just give me some water.

Deepak : Hey Kavita, why don't you come to my house these days?

Kavita : Deepak, you talk a lot of rubbish. I often come over.

Deepak : Okay Vrinda, give Kavita some tea.

Vrinda : I will bring the tea now. Until then you two talk.

1. दीपक की बहन का नाम क्या है? दीपक की बहन का नाम वृन्दा है।

2. क्या दीपक घर पर है? जी हाँ, दीपक घर पर है।

3. कविता क्या करती है? कविता डॉक्टरी पढ़ती है।

4. क्या आप कॉलेज में पढ़ते हैं? (पढ़ती हैं) जी हाँ, मैं कॉलेज में पढ़ता हूँ। (पढ़ती हूँ)

5. क्या आप काम करते हैं? (करती हैं) जी हाँ, मैं काम करता हूँ। (करती हूँ) जी नहीं, मैं काम नहीं करता। (करती)

6. कविता के कितने भाई-बहन हैं? कविता का एक भाई है।

7. आपके कितने भाई-बहन हैं? मेरा एक भाई है (दो भाई हैं) और एक बहन है (दो बहनें हैं)। मेरा भाई नहीं है।

8. कविता का भाई कहाँ रहता है? कविता का भाई ऑस्ट्रेलिया में रहता है।

9. आप कहाँ रहते हैं? (रहती हैं) मैं ... में रहता हूँ। (रहती हूँ)

10. क्या कविता अक्सर दीपक के घर आती है? जी हाँ, वह अक्सर आती है।

Lesson 10

Activity 10.1

1. हिन्दुस्तानी लड़के सुन्दर होते हैं । Indian boys are handsome.

2. छै और छै कितने होते हैं? How much is six and six?

3. आज बहुत गर्मी है । It is very hot today.

4. सिगरेट के धुएँ से खाँसी होती है । Cigarette smoke causes coughing.

5. भारत में बाघ होते हैं । Tigers occur in India.

6. अमरीका में किताबें महँगी हैं । Books are expensive in America.

7. भारत में मई के महीने में बहुत गर्मी होती है । It is hot in India in the month of May.

8. इंदिरा के बस्ते में एक क़लम है । There is a pen in Indira's bag.

9. इन नेताओं का भरोसा नहीं होता । These leaders are not to be trusted.

10. अधिक वर्षा से फ़सल ख़राब होती है । Crops are spoiled by too much rain.

11. वह हिन्दुस्तानी लड़की ख़ूबसूरत है । That Indian girl is beautiful.

12. इस नदी का पानी साफ़ नहीं है । The water in this river is not clean.

13. आम तौर पर हिन्दुस्तानी लोग बहुत उदार होते हैं ।

14. हिन्दी हिन्दुस्तान की एक भाषा है ।

15. दीपावली का त्यौहार नवम्बर में होता है ।

16. पवित्र गंगा का पानी साफ़ होता है ।

17. हिन्दी की कक्षा सोमवार को होती है ।

18. हर मंगल को हमारी छुट्टी होती है ।

19. मुहर्रम मुसलमानों का एक त्यौहार है ।

20. क्या हिन्दुस्तान के किसान बहुत ग़रीब हैं?

Activity 10.2

1. सोमवार को मैं कॉलेज जाता था । I (m) used to go to college on Monday(s).

2. उस लड़की के पिता जी हर साल हिन्दुस्तान जाते थे । That girl's father used to go to India every year.

3. आप किस जगह वकालत करती थीं? In which place did you use to practice law?

4. वह सुबह छह बजे उठता था । He used to get up at 6 o'clock in the morning.

5. जनवरी के महीने में माघ का मेला होता था । The Magh fair used to take place in the month of January.

6. इतवार को कोई अधिकारी बैंक में नहीं होता था । No official used to be in the bank on Sunday(s).

7. वे लड़कियाँ हिन्दी के अलावा और कुछ नहीं पढ़ती थीं । Those girls used to study nothing else apart from Hindi.

8. मैं अपने माँ-बाप से हिन्दी में ही बोलती थी । I (f) used to speak with my parents only in Hindi.

9. क्या तुम हर साल अपनी बहन के साथ भारत यात्रा करते थे? Did you (m) use to travel to India every year with your sister?

10. शाम को दुकानें बंद रहती थीं । The shops used to remain closed in the evening.

Activity 10.3

1. दीपक, अपनी किताब मुझे दो ।

2. आप अपनी तस्वीर उस के घर में लगाइए ।

3. रोज़ वह अपनी माँ के पास जाती है ।

4. आप मेरा नाम काग़ज़ पर लिखिये ।

5. देर से अपना काम मत देना ।

6. Study your Hindi every day.

7. That man used to tell his (own) life story.

8. Did you and your father use to go to the Magh fair in Allahabad?

9. That girl is independent (of her own mind).

10. Go to your room right now!

Activity 10.4: Conversation

Deepak : Kavita, did you use to live with your brother last year?

Kavita : No, but three years ago we used to live in Mumbai. My brother used to study there. Did you live in Delhi last year?

Deepak : No, we were in Allahabad. Our home is in Allahabad.

Kavita : Good. What is your sister's age?

Deepak : She is seventeen. What is your age, Kavita?

Kavita : I am twenty-two years old. And how old are you?

Deepak : I am also twenty-two years old.

Kavita : Good. The Magh fair takes place each year in Allahabad, doesn't it?

Deepak : Yes, a lot of people bathe in the Ganges and the Yamuna rivers.

Kavita : There is the confluence of the Ganges, the Yamuna and the Saraswati rivers there, isn't there?

Deepak : Yes, but the Saraswati flows underground. That's what people say.

Kavita : Did you use to bathe in the river with your sister?

Deepak : When we were children (in childhood) our mother would bathe us in the river. There is a great atmosphere in the Magh fair.

Kavita : Magh is the name of a month, right?

Deepak : Yes, the month of Magh is in January.

1. क्या तीन साल पहले कविता अपने भाई के साथ रहती थी? जी हाँ, तीन साल पहले कविता अपने भाई के साथ रहती थी।
2. क्या आप तीन साल पहले अपने भाई के साथ रहते थे? (रहती थीं) जी हाँ, तीन साल पहले अपने भाई के साथ मैं रहता था। (रहती थी) or जी नहीं, तीन साल पहले अपने भाई के साथ मैं नहीं रहता था। (नहीं रहती थी) or मेरा भाई नहीं है।
3. तीन साल पहले कविता कहाँ रहती थी? तीन साल पहले कविता मुम्बई में रहती थी।
4. तीन साल पहले आप कहाँ रहते थे? (रहती थीं) तीन साल पहले मैं ... में रहता था? (रहती थी)
5. कविता कितने साल की है? or कविता की उम्र क्या है? कविता बाईस साल की है। or कविता की उम्र बाईस साल की है।
6. आप की उम्र क्या है? or आप कितने साल के/की हैं? मेरी उम्र ... साल की है। or मैं ... साल का/की हूँ।
7. क्या बचपन में दीपक नदी में नहाता था? जी हाँ, बचपन में दीपक नदी में नहाता था (अपनी बहन के साथ)।
8. इलाहाबाद में कितनी नदियाँ मिलती हैं? इलाहाबाद में तीन नदियाँ मिलती हैं।

Lesson 11

Activity 11.1

1. Sit in that room and do your (own) work.
2. He and his mother used to go to Lucknow in the holidays.
3. Take my notebook out of your bag.
4. You (f) do your Hindi work yourself, don't you?
5. Why didn't he/they use to go there himself/themselves?
6. मैं अपना सब काम ख़ुद करता हूँ। (करती हूँ)
7. अपने-आप को आइने में देखो।
8. रजनीश अपने-आप को भगवान कहते थे।
9. तुम अपने-आप से बात क्यों करते हो? (करती हो)
10. दुनिया अपने-आप बदलती है।
11. यह दरवाज़ा अपने-आप खुलता है।

Activity 11.2

Once a boy used to live in Delhi. His name was Deepak. Often he would go to the market and from there go to his special friend Kavita's house. If his friend did not live so far then perhaps Deepak would have gone to her house every day. They would meet twice a week at the houses of their friends as well. His friend also would sometimes come to him. Both would have lengthy discussions (for a long time) about the country and society. The girl would say that if India's population weren't so great, then people's lives would be even better. Often she would even write letters to the government. But if the government actually listened to anyone, then perhaps there wouldn't have been so many problems.

1. लड़के का नाम दीपक था। The name of the boy was Deepak.

2. वह दिल्ली में रहता था। He used to live in Delhi.

3. लड़का कविता के घर अक्सर जाता था। The boy would often go to Kavita's home.

4. अगर कविता इतनी दूर नहीं रहती तो शायद लड़का उसके घर रोज़ जाता। If Kavita didn't live so far away, then perhaps the boy would have gone to her home every day.

5. दोनों देश और समाज के बारे में बातचीत करते थे। Both (of them) would talk about the country and society.

Activity 11.3

1. अगर वह कल रात को टेलीविज़न देखता तो वह एक हिन्दी फ़िल्म देखता।

2. अगर आज सुबह उसकी माँ आती तो वह उसे बाज़ार ले जाता।

3. अगर उस रात दीपक कविता को फूल देता तो शायद उनकी दोस्ती होती।

4. अगर इस मकान का किराया इतना नहीं होता तो मैं यहाँ रहता। (रहती)

Activity 11.4

1. रोज़ सुबह मैं सात बजे उठता हूँ। (उठती हूँ) I get up every day at 7 A.M.

2. पिछले साल मैं ... में रहता था। (रहती थी) Last year I used to live in ... .

3. हफ़्ते में रात को मैं ग्यारह बजे सोता हूँ। (सोती हूँ) During the week I sleep at 11 P.M.

4. वीक-एंड में रात को मैं बारह बजे सोता हूँ। (सोती हूँ) On the weekend I sleep at 12 A.M.

5. जी हाँ, मैं हर हफ़्ते सोमवार की सुबह शहर जाता हूँ। (जाती हूँ) or जी नहीं, मैं हर हफ़्ते सोमवार की सुबह शहर नहीं जाता। (जाती) Yes, every week I go to the city on Monday morning. or No, I don't go to the city every week on Monday morning.

6. मैं मंगल की सुबह आठ बजे नाश्ता करता हूँ। (करती हूँ) I eat breakfast on Tuesday(s) at 8 A.M.

7. रोज़ शाम को मैं चाय नहीं पीता। (नहीं पीती) or जी हाँ, रोज़ शाम को मैं चाय पीता हूँ। (पीती हूँ) I don't drink tea every evening. or Yes, I do drink tea every evening.

Activity 11.5: Conversation

Deepak : Kavita, whose CD do you want?

Kavita : I want a CD by Abida Parveen. I listen to her music a lot.

Deepak : Okay, let's look in this shop.

Kavita : Okay. This is a very old shop. My parents used to buy music stuff in this shop.

Deepak : What is Abida Parveen's music like? (what sort of music is hers)

Kavita : You don't know?

Deepak : If I knew about her, then would I ask this question?

Kavita : So buy a CD of hers and listen to it. She is famous throughout the whole world.

Deepak : Does she sing qawalis?

Kavita : Yes, she sings qawalis and ghazals. She often comes to India. If we knew each other last year then I would have taken you to her concert.

Deepak : That would have been great. Kavita, can you bargain in this shop?

Kavita : Deepak, this is not that kind of shop.

Deepak : If you could bargain here, then I would buy a lot.

Kavita : Deepak! You are so stingy. Don't you want a CD?

Deepak : Okay, I will buy a CD by Nusrat Fateh Ali Khan.

1. कविता किसका संगीत सुनती है? कविता आबिदा परबीन का संगीत सुनती है।

2. क्या यह संगीत की दुकान बहुत पुरानी है? जी हाँ, यह संगीत की दुकान बहुत पुरानी है।

3. अगर दीपक आबिदा परवीन के बारे में जानता तो क्या वह सवाल पूछता?

  अगर दीपक आबिदा परवीन के बारे में जानता तो वह सवाल नहीं पूछता।

4. क्या आप आबिदा परवीन का संगीत सुनते हैं? (सुनती हैं) जी हाँ, मैं आबिदा परवीन का संगीत

  सुनता हूँ। (सुनती हूँ) or जी नहीं, मैं आबिदा परवीन का संगीत नहीं सुनता। (नहीं सुनती)

5. क्या इस दुकान में मोलतोल होता है? जी नहीं, इस दुकान में मोलतोल नहीं होता।

6. अगर दुकान में मोलतोल होता तो क्या दीपक बहुत चीज़ें ख़रीदता?

  जी हाँ, अगर मोलतोल होता तो दीपक बहुत चीज़ें ख़रीदता।

7. दीपक किसकी सी० डी० ख़रीदता है? दीपक नुसरत फ़तह अली ख़ान की सी० डी० ख़रीदता है।

Lesson 12

Activity 12.1

1. वह रात को दस बजे सोयी। She slept at ten o'clock at night.

2. हम दिल्ली में रहे। We (*m*) lived in Delhi.

3. आप सोमवार को कहाँ गयीं? Where did you (*f*) go on Monday?

4. मैं अपना खाना लायी। I (*f*) brought my own food.

5. यह ठीक समय पर क्यों नहीं उठा? Why did he not get up on time?

6. गुरुवार को एक आदमी आया। A man came on Thursday.

7. सभी भाषाएँ क्यों बदलीं? Why did all the languages change?

8. तुम कॉलेज कितने बजे पहुँचे? What time did you (*m*) arrive at college?

9. क्या आपकी बातें उससे हुईं? Did you talk to him/her?

10. दुकानें नौ बजे खुलीं। The stores opened at 9 o'clock.

Activity 12.2

1. वह दुकान में गया और उसने कुछ सब्ज़ियाँ ख़रीदीं।

2. हमने क्लास में प्रेमचंद की एक कहानी पढ़ी।

3. कल मैंने अपने दोस्त के साथ एक अच्छी फ़िल्म देखी।

4. पिछले हफ़्ते कक्षा में क्या हुआ?

5. वह कक्षा में अपनी सहेली को लायी।

6. आज सुबह मेरा भाई छै बजे उठा।

7. वह उस दिन अपनी बहनों की सहेली से विश्वविद्यालय में मिला।

8. मैं अभी आया।

9. "ॐ शांति ॐ" नामक फ़िल्म किसने देखी?

10. कल रात को आपने क्या किया?

Activity 12.3: Conversation

Kavita   : Hello Deepak, how are you?

Deepak   : Hey Kavita. Come in. Where were you for the past so many days?

Kavita   : I was in Lucknow. Have you ever been to Lucknow?

Deepak   : I have never been. Why did you go to Lucknow?

Kavita   : My father often has some work in Lucknow. So he goes there sometimes. I also went with him this time.

Deepak   : So what did you do in Lucknow?

Kavita   : I just relaxed. I slept in till late in the morning. Some of our relatives live in Lucknow. We stayed with them. I also went to see the Bara Imambara with them.

Deepak   : What's the Bara Imambara?

Kavita   : It is a very beautiful building. A Nawab had it built.

Deepak : Don't you know the name of the Nawab?

Kavita : Yes, I know. His name was Asaf-ud-Daula. He had the Bara Imambara built in the eighteenth century. He was a very generous Nawab.

Deepak : Wow, you learned a lot about Lucknow. So what else did you do in Lucknow?

Kavita : Not much. It was the festival of Eid. So we went to the house of some friends of our relatives.

Deepak : What do people do on the day of Eid?

Kavita : I would tell you if I had time right now.

1. पिछले हफ़्ते कविता कहाँ थी? पिछले हफ़्ते कविता लखनऊ में थी।

2. क्या दीपक कभी लखनऊ गया? दीपक कभी लखनऊ नहीं गया।

3. क्या आप कभी लखनऊ गये? (गयीं) जी हाँ, मैं लखनऊ गया। (गयी) or
   जी नहीं, मैं लखनऊ कभी नहीं गया। (नहीं गयी)

4. क्या आप कभी हिन्दुस्तान गये? (गयीं) जी हाँ, मैं हिन्दुस्तान गया। (गयी) or
   जी नहीं, मैं हिन्दुस्तान कभी नहीं गया। (नहीं गयी)

5. क्या कविता के पिता जी कभी कभी लखनऊ जाते हैं? जी हाँ, कविता के पिता जी कभी कभी लखनऊ जाते हैं।

6. क्या कविता अपने रिश्तेदारों के साथ लखनऊ में रही? जी हाँ, कविता अपने रिश्तेदारों के साथ लखनऊ में रही।

7. क्या आप हिन्दुस्तान में अपने रिश्तेदारों के साथ रहते हैं? (रहती हैं) जी हाँ, मैं अपने रिश्तेदारों
   के साथ रहता हूँ। (रहती हूँ) or जी नहीं, हिन्दुस्तान में मेरा कोई रिश्तेदार नहीं है।

8. क्या कविता अपने रिश्तेदारों के साथ उनके दोस्तों के घर गयी? जी हाँ, कविता अपने रिश्तेदारों के साथ उनके दोस्तों के
   घर गयी।

Lesson 13

Activity 13.1

1. क्या इस साल आप के पास गाड़ी है? Do you have a car this year?

2. अभी उस के पास कितने पैसे हैं? How much money does he/she have right now?

3. मेरी माँ की दो बहनें हैं। My mother has two sisters.

4. हमारे घर में दो कमरे हैं। Our house has two rooms.

5. उस मामले में इसके क्या विचार थे? What were his/her thoughts on this matter?

6. अभी मेरी मदद करने के लिये क्या शिक्षक के पास समय है? Does the teacher have time right now to help me?

7. बताइये, आपके कितने सवाल हैं? Tell (me), how many questions do you have?

8. भारतीय महिला के क्या-क्या विशेष गुण होते हैं? What special virtues does an Indian woman possess?

9. उनको किताबें पढ़ने का शौक है। He/she/they enjoy(s) reading books.

10. क्या आप में हिम्मत है? Do you have courage?

11. वह एक बहुत बड़े पेड़ के पास खड़ा था। He was standing near a very big tree.

12. सीधे डॉक्टर के पास इलाज के लिये जाओ। Go straight to the doctor for treatment.

13. घड़ी में दो सुइयाँ होती थीं। A watch used to have two hands.

14. कक्षा में आपके पास कौन बैठता है? Who sits near you in class?

15. क्या दीपक की कुछ ज़मीन थी? Did Deepak have some land?

Activity 13.2

1. क्या खाने (के लिये/को/...) आपके पास पैसे हैं?

2. क्या तैरने (के लिये/को/...) उसके पास समय था?

3. क्या आपने सरदर्द दूर करने (के लिये/को/...) उसे गोली दी?

4. क्या तुमने हिन्दुस्तान (भारत) जाने (के लिये/को/...) उन्हें पैसे दिये?

5. उसके पास पढ़ने (के लिये/को/...) कोई किताब नहीं है।

6. साल के अंत में हिन्दी पढ़ने (के लिये/को/...) भारत आइये।

7. भारत में हिन्दी सीखना ज़्यादा अच्छा है।

8. फ़िल्म देखने (के लिये/को/...) शहर आओ/आना/आइए।

9. हम सामान लेने (के लिये/को/...) बाज़ार गये।

Activity 13.3

1. क्या आपने ये किताबें ख़रीदी हैं? Have you bought these books?

2. तुम (*m*) मेरी कुर्सी पर क्यों बैठे हो? Why are you sitting on my chair?

3. उस की शादी किसी भारतीय महिला से हुई है। He has married an Indian woman.

4. हम (*f*) दोबारा भारत आयी हैं। We have come to India a second time.

5. उन्होंने अभी-अभी अपना काम पूरा किया है। They have just finished their work.

6. वह (*m*) भारत से अमरीका दो हफ़्ते के लिये आया है। He has come to America from India for two weeks.

7. क्या आपने ये किताबें ख़रीदी थीं? Had you bought these books?

8. तुम (*m*) मेरी कुर्सी पर क्यों बैठे थे? Why were you (*m*) seated on my chair?

9. उस की शादी किसी भारतीय महिला से हुई थी। He had married an Indian woman.

10. हम (*f*) दोबारा भारत आयी थीं। We had come to India a second time.

11. उन्होंने अभी-अभी अपना काम पूरा किया था। They had just finished their work.

12. वह (*m*) भारत से अमरीका दो हफ़्ते के लिये आया था। He had come to America from India for two weeks.

Activity 13.4: Conversation

Deepak : Kavita, do you want to go to Old Delhi to eat today?

Kavita : Not today. Why don't we go to Bengali Market? I haven't gone there for many days.

Deepak : I had gone there two days ago. But, okay, we (will) go there. The *chat* there is very good.

Kavita : Yes, and I had read in the newspaper last week that a new *chat* shop has opened there. I have heard that their potato patties are really worth eating. People say that the new shop's food is really spicy and tasty.

Deepak : That's fine. But I want to eat in the Bengali Sweet House.

Kavita : I have eaten there so many times. Why don't we go to a new place?

Deepak : Okay. How much time do you have?

Kavita : I have about one hour. I will phone my mother to tell her what we are doing (what the program is).

Deepak : Okay. Do you have a car today?

Kavita : No, I have come by the metro today.

Deepak : Okay, no problem (no matter). I have a car. Okay, let's go now.

1. आज दीपक खाना खाने कहाँ जाना चाहता है? आज दीपक पुरानी दिल्ली खाना खाने जाना चाहता है।

2. क्या आज रात को आप बाहर खाना खाने जाना चाहते हैं?
(चाहती हैं) जी हाँ, मैं बाहर जाना चाहता हूँ। (चाहती हूँ)

3. क्या आज कविता पुरानी दिल्ली खाने को जाना चाहती है? जी नहीं वह बंगाली मार्केट जाना चाहती है।

4. कितने दिन पहले दीपक बंगाली मार्केट गया था? दो दिन पहले दीपक बंगाली मार्केट गया था।

5. क्या बंगाली मार्केट में चाट आम तौर पर बहुत अच्छी होती है?
जी हाँ, बंगाली मार्केट में चाट आम तौर पर बहुत अच्छी होती है।

6. पिछले हफ़्ते कविता ने अख़बार में क्या पढ़ा था?
पिछले हफ़्ते कविता ने अख़बार में पढ़ा था कि बंगाली मार्केट में एक नयी दुकान खुली है।

7. बंगाली मार्केट की नयी दुकान के बारे में लोग क्या कहते हैं? बंगाली मार्केट की नयी दुकान के बारे में लोग कहते हैं कि नयी दुकान का खाना बहुत चटपटा और मज़ेदार होता है।

8. कविता के पास कितना समय है? कविता के पास लगभग एक घंटा है।

9. क्या आज कविता मेट्रो से यूनिवर्सिटी आयी है? जी हाँ, आज कविता मेट्रो से यूनिवर्सिटी आयी है।

10. क्या आज दीपक के पास गाड़ी है? जी हाँ, आज दीपक के पास गाड़ी है।

Lesson 14

Activity 14.1

1. मैं (*m*) अभी घर जा रहा हूँ। I am going home right now.

2. हम (*m*) अभी एक दोस्त के घर में हिन्दी सीख रहे हैं। We are learning Hindi at a friend's home right now.

3. तो तू (*f*) अभी क्या कर रही है? So, what are you doing right now?

4. तुम (*m*) यही किताब क्यों पढ़ रहे हो? Why are you reading *this* book?

5. आप (*f*) अभी किस को चिट्ठी लिख रही हैं? To whom are you writing a letter right now?

6. आज भी बहुत ठंड (*f*) हो रही है। It is very cold today as well.

7. वह लड़का तो कमरे में दूध पी रहा है। That boy is drinking milk in the room.

8. सभी लड़कियाँ ऊपर तो नहीं सो रही हैं। Not all of the girls are sleeping upstairs.

Activity 14.2

1. कल ही दिन में मैं (*f*) यह काम कर रही थी। Just yesterday during the day I was doing this work.

2. कल रात को भी वह पुस्तकालय में पढ़ रहा था। Last night as well, he was reading in the library.

3. उस समय हम बग़ीचे में टहल रहे थे। We were strolling in the garden at that time.

4. कल दो बजे उससे बातें हो रही थीं। Yesterday at two o'clock talks were taking place with him/her.

5. तभी यह लड़की खिड़की खोल रही थी। Right then this girl was opening the window.

6. जी, मेरे पिता जी उस समय उस दुकान में कुछ सामान ख़रीद रहे थे। Sir, my father was buying some things in that shop at that time.

7. वहीं कुछ आदमी खाना खा रहे थे। Some men were eating food right there.

Activity 14.3

1. जी नहीं, मैं हिन्दुस्तान ही जाता हूँ। (जाती हूँ)

2. जी नहीं, मैं हिन्दी बोलता भी हूँ। (बोलती भी हूँ)

3. जी नहीं, मैं ही गाड़ी चलाता हूँ। (चलाती हूँ)

4. जी नहीं, मैं हिन्दी भी पढ़ता हूँ। (पढ़ती हूँ।)

5. जी नहीं, मैं भी हिन्दी लिखता हूँ। (लिखती हूँ)

Activity 14.4

1. क्या आप विश्वविद्यालय में पढ़ते हैं? (पढ़ती हैं)

2. जी हाँ, मैं विश्वविद्यालय में पढ़ता हूँ। (पढ़ती हूँ)

3. क्या आप कभी विश्वविद्यालय गये हैं? (गई हैं)

4. जी हाँ, मैं विश्वविद्यालय गया हूँ। (गई हूँ)

5. क्या आप अभी विश्वविद्यालय जा रहे हैं? (जा रही हैं)

6. जी नहीं, मैं अभी विश्वविद्यालय नहीं जा रहा हूँ। (नहीं जा रही हूँ)

7. क्या कल आप विश्वविद्यालय गये? (गई)

8. जी हाँ, मैं कल विश्वविद्यालय गया। (गई)

9. क्या कल तीन बजे आप विश्वविद्यालय जा रहे थे? (जा रही थीं)

10. जी नहीं, मैं कल तीन बजे विश्वविद्यालय नहीं जा रहा था। (नहीं जा रही थी)

11. मैं अपनी माँ के घर जा रहा था। (जा रही थी)

12. क्या पिछले हफ़्ते आप विश्वविद्यालय गये थे? (गई थीं)

13. जी नहीं, पिछले हफ़्ते छुट्टी थी।

14. अगर आज आप विश्वविद्यालय जाते (जाती) तो क्या आप पुस्तकालय में जाते? (जातीं)

15. जी हाँ, अगर आज मैं विश्वविद्यालय जाता (जाती) तो मैं पुस्तकालय में जाता। (जातीं)

16. क्या पिछले साल आप विश्वविद्यालय जाते थे? (जाती थीं)

17. जी नहीं, पिछले साल मैं विश्वविद्यालय नहीं जाता था। (नहीं जाती थी)

Activity 14.5: Conversation

Deepak : Hey Kavita, what are you doing here right now?

Kavita : I have come to buy some things with my mom. Mom has gone into a store. Why (do you ask)?

Deepak : I am going to pick up my father from the station right now. I am going in my car. (Why don't you) go with me.

Kavita : Really, your father is coming?

Deepak : Yes, he is coming from Allahabad.

Kavita : Why didn't you tell me? Okay, I too (will) come. One minute, I will tell mom. By which train is your father coming?

Deepak : By the Prayag Express. It gets in at three o'clock in the afternoon.

Kavita : Then we only have half an hour. Let's go (move).

Deepak : Why didn't you go to college yesterday? What were you doing?

Kavita : I had gone (I went), *ji*! I was reading a book in the afternoon in the library. What were you doing at that time?

Deepak : I too was at college. I needed one of your books.

Kavita : Really, then why didn't you come into the library to search for me?

Deepak : I did (had gone). But I didn't see you. Okay, the station is in front. Let's go to platform number three.

Kavita : The train is over there. Look in front.

Deepak : Yes, yes. And I can see (my) dad (father is visible). He is waving (his hand). He has seen us.

1. अभी कविता क्या कर रही है? अभी कविता माँ के साथ कुछ सामान ख़रीदने बाज़ार आयी है।

2. अभी आप क्या कर रहे हैं? (कर रही हैं) अभी मैं हिन्दी पढ़ रहा हूँ। (पढ़ रही हूँ)

3. कविता किस के साथ बाज़ार आयी है? कविता अपनी माँ के साथ बाज़ार आयी है।

4. अभी दीपक कहाँ जा रहा है? अभी दीपक स्टेशन जा रहा है।

5. दीपक स्टेशन क्यों जा रहा है? दीपक अपने पिता जी को लेने (के लिए/को/...) स्टेशन जा रहा है।

6. इलाहाबाद से कौन आ रहा है? इलाहाबाद से दीपक के पिता जी आ रहे हैं।

7. क्या कविता कल कॉलेज गयी थी? जी हाँ, कल वह कॉलेज गयी थी।

8. कल दीपक को क्या चाहिए था? कल दीपक को कविता की एक किताब चाहिए थी।

9. रेलगाड़ी किस प्लैटफ़ार्म पर आ रही है? रेलगाड़ी तीन नम्बर प्लैटफ़ार्म पर आ रही है।

Lesson 15

Activity 15.1

1. If he lived with us, then we (*m*) would have taught him about our country.

2. If he had lived with us, then we (*m*) would have taught him about our country.

3. If he/she was able to understand this thing right now, then I (*f*) would have helped him/her.

4. If you (*m*) had gone to India, then your Hindi would have been very good.

5. If he (*m*) had come to university, then he too would have seen this Hindi film.

6. If you (*f*) bathed in the Ganges river, then all of your sins would have been erased.

7. If you had not asked this question, then I (*f*) would not have thought about that matter.

8. If they/she read this article, then they/she would have known something about Gandhi *ji*.

9. If you had bought a pen, then this difficulty would not have happened in the exam.

10. If you had invited (called) me, then I (*m*) would have come to you.

11. If I had money, then I (*m*) too would eat *gulabjamuns*.

12. If my brother drank sherbert, then his thirst would have been quenched.

13. If you did all of your work, then you would have passed the exam.

14. (अगर/यदि) मैंने यह किताब पढ़ी होती तो मैं आपको देता। (देती)

Note that numbers 14 to 19 can have several other possible alternatives depending on the context. For example, number 16 with a masculine subject could be expressed:

(अगर/यदि) मेरी गाड़ी ख़राब न होती तो मैं उसे चलाता।

(अगर/यदि) मेरी गाड़ी ख़राब न होती तो मैंने उसे चलाया होता।

(अगर/यदि) मेरी गाड़ी ख़राब न हुई होती तो मैं उसे चलाता।

(अगर/यदि) मेरी गाड़ी ख़राब न हुई होती तो मैंने उसे चलाया होता।

नहीं can also be substituted for न।

15. (अगर/यदि) आपके पास वक़्त होता तो मुझे अस्पताल में देखने (के लिये/को/...) आते। (आतीं)

16. (अगर/यदि) मेरी गाड़ी ख़राब न होती तो मैं उसे चलाता। (चलाती)

17. (अगर/यदि) कविता ने खाना पकाया होता तो परिवार के लोग खाते।

18. (अगर/यदि) मैं हिन्दी न पढ़ता तो मैं बंगला पढ़ता। (पढ़ती)

19. (अगर/यदि) वे अभी लाइब्रेरी में पढ़ाई कर रहे होते तो मैं उनकी तलाश करता। (करता)

Activity 15.2

1. क्या कोई औरत उस कमरे में खड़ी है? (जी हाँ)

2. क्या मैं हिन्दुस्तान के बारे में कुछ जानता हूँ? (जी नहीं)

3. क्या आपके साथ कुछ लोग हिन्दी पढ़ते हैं? (जी हाँ)

4. क्या आप के साथ कोई और हिन्दी नहीं पढ़ता था? (पढ़ती थीं) (जी हाँ)

5. क्या आप के दोस्त ने पिछले साल आप के साथ कुछ हिन्दी पढ़ी थी? (जी हाँ)

6. क्या छात्र व्याकरण के बारे में सब कुछ सीखना चाहते हैं? (जी नहीं)

7. क्या और कोई अभी शहर आ रहा है? (जी नहीं)

8. क्या आपके प्याले में कुछ चाय है? (जी हाँ)

9. क्या किसी को मदद चाहिये? (जी हाँ)

Activity 15.3

1. अपना काम कर के वह बाहर गया। He did his work and went outside.

2. हम शहर जाकर फ़िल्में देखते हैं। We go to the city and watch films.

3. मेरे कमरे में आकर इस कुर्सी पर बैठिये। Come into my room and sit on this chair.

4. तुम (*m*) दो किताबें लेकर आये थे। You (*m*) had come with two books.

5. उस छात्रा ने हिन्दुस्तान जाकर हिन्दी सीखी। That student (*f*) went to India and learned Hindi.

6. मेरी माँ मेरे कपड़े लेकर अपने घर गयी। My mother took my clothes to her house.

7. सभी लोग ध्यान देकर शिक्षिका की बात सुनते थे। Everyone used to listen to the teacher (*f*) with attention.

8. लोग इलाहाबाद जाकर गंगा में नहाते थे। People used to go to Allahabad and bathe in the Ganges.

9. मुझे मेरी किताब देकर जाओ। Give me my book and go.

10. उसको चिट्ठी लिखकर सभी बातें बताना। Write him/her a letter and tell (him/her) everything.

Activity 15.4: Conversation

Deepak : Kavita, you didn't tell me anything about Eid.

Kavita : Okay, I (will) tell you. Eid is a very important festival for Muslims. The story of Eid is also very old. (They) celebrate Eid several times in the year.

Deepak : So tell me, which Eid is this?

Kavita : Some people call this Eid-uz-Juha, then some call it Eid-ul-Azha. But ordinarily children call this Baqra Eid. At this festival people sacrifice an animal, pray in the mosque and remember God.

Deepak : Lucknow is famous for its Nawabi culture, isn't it?

Kavita : Yes, and at the time of Eid, the atmosphere there is grand.

Deepak : Really! If I had gone to Lucknow, I too would have seen all of this.

Kavita : Next time come with us and see Lucknow.

Deepak : Tell me some more about Lucknow, Kavita.

Kavita : If I weren't on my way home right now, then I would tell (you) several things. But right now I don't have time.

Deepak : Come tomorrow and tell me the rest of the story.

Kavita : Okay. Okay Deepak, I'm off now. Bye.

1. क्या कविता दीपक को ईद के बारे में बताती है? जी हाँ, वह दीपक को ईद के बारे में कुछ बताती है।

2. अगर दीपक लखनऊ गया होता तो क्या वह ईद मनाता? जी हाँ, अगर दीपक लखनऊ गया होता तो वह ईद मनाता।

3. क्या ईद के दिन लोग मस्जिद जाकर नमाज़ पढ़ते हैं? जी हाँ, ईद के दिन लोग मस्जिद जाकर नमाज़ पढ़ते हैं।

4. क्या आप लखनऊ जाकर ईद मनाना चाहते हैं? (चाहती हैं) जी हाँ, मैं लखनऊ जाकर ईद मनाना चाहता हूँ। (चाहती हूँ)

5. अगर कविता अभी घर नहीं जा रही होती तो क्या वह पूरी कहानी सुनाती? जी हाँ, अगर कविता अभी घर नहीं जा रही होती तो वह पूरी कहानी सुनाती।

6. क्या ईद की कहानी बहुत पुरानी है? जी हाँ, वह बहुत पुरानी है।

7. लखनऊ में कविता ने कौन-सी ईद मनायी थी? लखनऊ में कविता ने बक्रईद मनायी थी।

Lesson 16

Activity 16.1

1. शायद मैं यह किताब पढ़ूँ। Perhaps I may read this book.

2. संभव है कि वह हिन्दी सीखकर भारत जाए। It is possible that he/she may learn Hindi and go to India.

3. हिन्दुस्तान जा कर हम क्या करें? What should we do in India? (having gone to India)

4. शायद इस साल छात्र परीक्षा में अच्छा काम करें। Perhaps the students will do well in the exam this year. (give a good exam)

5. उस की इच्छा है कि उस के सिर पर काम का बोझ न हो। It is his/her desire that he/she not be burdened with work.

6. मैं चाहता हूँ कि आप सभी लोग परीक्षा में सफल हों। I want you all to be successful in the exam.

7. शायद वह आप की मदद करे। Perhaps he/she may help you.

8. जल्दी पढ़ाई ख़त्म करो ताकि तुम फ़िल्म देखने जाओ। Finish your studies quickly so that you may go to watch a film.

9. बेटे, तुम ख़ुश रहो। Son, may you remain happy.

10. कृपया मुझे चिट्ठी लिख कर भेजें। Please be kind enough to write (and send) me a letter.

Activity 16.2

1. आज शायद शिक्षक तुम्हारे दोस्त से बात कर रहे थे।

2. हो सकता है कि उसने अपना हिन्दी का काम ख़तम किया हो।

3. मैं सोचता हूँ (सोचती हूँ) कि शायद वह अपनी माँ को ले कर हिन्दुस्तान गयी हो।

4. मैं सोचता हूँ (सोचती हूँ) कि शायद मैंने यह फ़िल्म देखी हो।

5. शायद वह अभी छात्रों से बात कर रही हो।

6. शायद उन्होंने अब तक न खाया हो।

7. शायद ये छात्र पुस्तकालय में पढ़ते हों।

8. शायद उसने चिट्ठी लिखकर भेजी हो।

9. शायद वह हर साल हिन्दुस्तान जाती हो।

Activity 16.3: Conversation

Deepak   : Hi Kavita, come in(side). How are you?

Kavita   : Fine. What about you?

Deepak   : Everything is going just okay.

Kavita   : Did your father return to Allahabad?

Deepak   : Yes, yes. He went last week. He said that I should certainly take you there. (You take Kavita and come to Allahabad) Have you ever been to Allahabad?

Kavita   : Nope, I have never been. So, shall we take a trip to Allahabad? (shall we wander [in] Allahabad and come)

Deepak   : Yes. I wanted to ask you but I thought that perhaps you may have too much work at this time.

Kavita   : Certainly not. Where did you get that idea? My exams finished two weeks ago. These days I have plenty of time.

Deepak   : That's great. Shall I speak to your parents about going?

Kavita   : Why do you need to do this? (what need is there of this) My folks have no such objections. Perhaps my mom is doing some work at home right now. Shall I phone her and ask?

Deepak   : Certainly. You phone (her) right now and I will make two cups of tea.

1. क्या दीपक के पिता जी इलाहाबाद वापस गये हैं? जी हाँ, वे वापस गये हैं।
2. दीपक के पिता जी इलाहाबाद कब वापस गये थे? दीपक के पिता जी पिछले हफ्ते इलाहाबाद वापस गये थे।
3. क्या कविता कभी इलाहाबाद गयी है? जी नहीं, वह कभी नहीं गयी।
4. क्या यह संभव है कि दीपक और कविता इलाहाबाद जाएँ? जी हाँ, यह संभव है कि दीपक और कविता इलाहाबाद जाएँ।
5. क्या यह मुमकिन है कि तुम इलाहाबाद जाओ? जी हाँ, यह मुमकिन है कि मैं इलाहाबाद जाऊँ। or जी नहीं, यह मुमकिन नहीं है कि मैं इलाहाबाद जाऊँ।
6. दीपक क्या बनाकर लाता है? दीपक चाय बनाकर लाता है।
7. क्या यह हो सकता है कि आप दीपक के साथ इलाहाबाद जाएँ? जी हाँ, यह हो सकता है कि मैं दीपक के साथ इलाहाबाद जाऊँ। or जी नहीं, यह नहीं हो सकता कि मैं दीपक के साथ इलाहाबाद जाऊँ।

Lesson 17

Activity 17.1

1. अगले हफ्ते मैं भारत जाऊँगी।
2. कल हम कक्षा में आयेंगे।
3. क्या आप आज रात को टी० वी० देखेंगे? (देखेंगी)
4. सोमवार को सुबह वह मुझे/मुझको फ़ोन करेगी।
5. अगले साल वह हिन्दुस्तान जाकर हिन्दी पढ़ेगा।
6. परसों हमारी परीक्षा होगी।
7. उन्होंने कहा कि वे इस बात के बारे में सोचेंगे।
8. मंगलवार को मैं कुछ नहीं करूँगा। (करूँगी)
9. शनिवार को वह शहर जाकर एक फ़िल्म देखेगी।
10. मेरा दोस्त आपके लिये कुछ कपड़े हिन्दुस्तान से लाएगा।
11. We will not drink alcohol.
12. You (*m*) will go only after having finished your work.
13. She will bring these things from her place to my house, won't she?
14. I (*m*) will give your watch to the watchmaker to fix.
15. Will our class take place in (after) two weeks, or not?
16. Will you (*f*) help me in the future?
17. Perhaps he will write you a letter from India.
18. The hearing will happen in court next week.
19. Tomorrow we will talk about this on the phone.
20. You (people) will only be successful in the exam having worked hard.

Activity 17.2

1. वह अपने कमरे में काम कर रही होगी।
2. दीपक अभी यूनिवर्सिटी आता होगा।
3. यह भी ठीक होगा।
4. अभी तक उसने अपना काम ख़त्म किया होगा।
5. वे अभी लाइब्रेरी में हिन्दी पढ़ रहे होंगे।
6. तुम छै बजे तक उठते होगे। (उठती होगी)
7. शायद अभी तक वह नहीं गया होगा।
8. इसका दाम बहुत होगा।
9. छात्र अपने शिक्षक से हिन्दी में बोलते होंगे।
10. यह दस साल पहले हुआ होगा।
11. Their class must take place on Monday(s).
12. She must go to university on Tuesday(s).
13. This incident must have happened on Wednesday.
14. All of the students must have gone to India on Thursday.
15. Don't disturb her. She must be working.

Activity 17.3

1. (तुम) उसे हिन्दुस्तान का सफ़र करने दो। Let him/her travel to India.
2. देखना कि चोर न भागने पाये। Look (so) that the thief may not escape.
3. मेरी ओर देखकर वह फ़ोन रखने लगी। She began to put down the phone when she saw me.
4. फ़िल्म देख कर हम अपने बारे में सोचने लगे। We began to think about ourselves after we saw the film.
5. उन्हें यहाँ बैठने दें। Please let them/him/her sit here.
6. शायद मैं तुम्हें हिन्दुस्तान जा कर हिन्दी सीखने दूँ।
7. दरवाज़ा खोलकर वह अन्दर आने लगा।
8. सोमवार को हम एक नयी कहानी पढ़ने लगेंगे।
9. माँ को लेकर वह हिन्दुस्तान जाने नहीं पाएगी।
10. वे लोगों के बीच में खड़े होकर भाषण देने लगे।

Activity 17.4

1. If you may come to university, please meet with me.
2. Where will I find a cobbler here?
3. How much do you earn a month?
4. Janpath intersects with Rajpath.
5. Perhaps I (f) may have met you at some time.
6. Last week he/she ran into his/her (own) friend (f) in the city.
7. It will be great if I get a job.

Activity 17.5: Conversation

Deepak : Mom, where is dad?

Vimla : He has gone to the market to get some things.

Deepak : Mom, have you ever met Kavita?

Vimla : Perhaps we have met. Where do you live, (my) daughter?

Kavita : *Ji*, I live in Delhi. Have you ever been to Delhi?

Vimla : No, (my) daughter.

Kavita : Then we must not have met before because prior to this I have never been to Allahabad.

Vimla : You must study with Deepak, right?

Kavita	: Yes, but from next year I will undertake medical studies. I want to treat children.
Vimla	: That will be great. Deepak, you are going to become a journalist, aren't you?
Deepak	: I will try to become (one). I have already begun to write some articles. One of my articles was even published in the newspaper.
Vimla	: Great. You both go and sit in the living room. I will make some tea. Your father must be on his way.
Kavita	: What's there to see in Allahabad?
Vimla	: Well, there's the confluence. You must have heard about that. Deepak's father will take you both and show it to you.
Kavita	: Can we also bathe in the river?
Vimla	: If you want to bathe, then certainly. But the water will/must be very cold.

1. क्या दीपक और कविता इलाहाबाद गये हैं? जी हाँ, वे इलाहाबाद गये हैं।
2. दीपक के पिता जी बाज़ार क्यों गये हैं? वे कुछ सामान लाने बाज़ार गए हैं।
3. क्या पहले कविता दीपक की माँ से कभी मिली होगी? जी नहीं, वह उनसे कभी नहीं मिली होगी।
4. क्या कविता दीपक के साथ पढ़ती होगी? जी हाँ, वह दीपक के साथ पढ़ती होगी।
5. क्या दीपक कहानियाँ लिखने लगा है? जी नहीं, वह लेख लिखने लगा है।
6. क्या आप कभी दीपक के माँ-बाप से मिले हैं? (मिली हैं) जी नहीं, मैं उनसे कभी नहीं मिला हूँ। (मिली हूँ)
7. क्या आप इलाहाबाद जाकर दीपक के माँ-बाप से मिलेंगे? (मिलेंगी) जी हाँ, मैं इलाहाबाद जाकर उनसे मिलूँगा। (मिलूँगी)
8. क्या दीपक और कविता बैठक में जाकर चाय पिएँगे? जी हाँ, वे बैठक में जाकर चाय पिएँगे।
9. क्या आजकल गंगा का पानी बहुत ठंडा होगा? जी हाँ, वह आजकल बहुत ठंडा होगा।

Lesson 18

Activity 18.1

1. He/she/they must become quite angry.
2. But it also seems that he/she/they is/are very afraid.
3. But I hope that one day he/she/they finds/find peace.
4. Because if he/she/they doesn't/don't find peace, then he/she/they will remain very bothered.
5. You will find out the reality of life.
6. Just yesterday I found out that it costs a lot to go to India.
7. But you will like going there.
8. Who knows Hindi?
9. I am *so* hungry.
10. Perhaps it may take four hours to go to New York by bus.
11. आपको ऐसा लगता होगा कि मुझे फल खाना अच्छा नहीं लगता।
12. उसे पुस्तकालय में हिन्दी की किताबें पढ़ना बहुत अच्छा लगता था।
13. मुझे ऐसा लगता है कि आपके पास कुछ भी पैसे नहीं होंगे।
14. मेधा को चाय पीना बहुत अच्छा लगता है।
15. चिट्ठी लिखने में सिर्फ़ बीस मिनट लगते हैं।

Activity 18.2

1. एक पाठ पूरा करने में मुझको एक हफ़्ता लगता है।
2. हवाई जहाज़ से हिन्दुस्तान जाने में दो दिन लगते होंगे।
3. शहर से उसके घर पहुँचने में चालीस मिनट लगने लगे हैं।
4. सच्चाई पता चलने में बहुत देर लगेगी।
5. दूसरी भाषा सीखने में कुछ साल लगते हैं।
6. हिन्दुस्तान जाने में शायद बहुत पैसे लगें।
7. आटा गूँधने में बहुत मेहनत लगती है।

Activity 18.3

1. What were you doing yesterday at 3:30 P.M.? कल दोपहर को साढ़े तीन बजे मैं कुछ काम कर रहा था। (कर रही थी) Yesterday at 3:30 P.M. I was doing some work.

2. Will you come to my home tomorrow at 12:45 P.M.? जी हाँ, मैं कल दोपहर को पौन बजे आप के घर आऊँगा (आऊँगी) Yes, I will come to your home tomorrow at 12:45 P.M.

3. Were you reading a book yesterday at 2:30? जी हाँ, कल ढाई बजे मैं किताब पढ़ रहा था। (पढ़ रही थी) Yes, I was reading a book yesterday at 2:30. जी नहीं, कल ढाई बजे मैं किताब नहीं पढ़ रहा था (नहीं पढ़ रही थी), मैं एक दोस्त से बात कर रहा था। (कर रही थी) No, yesterday at 2:30 I was not reading a book, I was talking to a friend.

4. Do you eat lunch at 1:30 P.M. every day? जी हाँ, मैं रोज़ दोपहर को डेढ़ बजे दिन का खाना खाता हूँ। (खाती हूँ) Yes, I eat lunch every day at 1:30 P.M. जी नहीं, मैं रोज़ दोपहर को साढ़े बारह बजे दिन का खाना खाता हूँ। (खाती हूँ) No, I eat lunch every day at 12:30 P.M.

5. Were you asleep until 10:15 this morning? जी हाँ, आज सुबह सवा दस बजे तक मैं सोया था। (सोयी थी) Yes, I was asleep until 10:15 this morning. जी नहीं, आज सुबह सवा दस बजे मैं उठा था। (उठी थी) No, I was up at 10:15 this morning.

Activity 18.4: Conversation

Deepak : Hello Kavita. What are you doing right now?

Kavita : I am going to class. What's the time? (how many have struck)

Deepak : It is now 2:30 P.M. Do you know that a new film has come out?

Kavita : No, I didn't know. What's its name?

Deepak : *I Too Am (Here)*. Shall we go to see it?

Kavita : Perhaps I may go. Which day and what time are you going?

Deepak : I am going to see the 6 o'clock show on Saturday with some friends.

Kavita : I will think about it. I am not a big fan of such films.

Deepak : How do you know that the film won't be good? I heard that it is very good.

Kavita : Okay. I am so hungry. Do you want to grab a cup of tea with me before my class?

Deepak : I don't really like the tea here. But I like the coffee. So I will have a coffee. Didn't you eat anything for lunch? (during the day)

Kavita : I didn't have time. I have a class at twelve o'clock. And it takes me a full two hours to come to college in the morning. I am always late getting here.

Deepak : Okay, so are you coming to watch the film on Saturday or not?

Kavita : Okay, *baba*. I will go. When and what time will we meet?

Deepak : Come to my house at 4:30 in the evening. We will go from there.

Kavita : Good. Now I am off to class. See you on Saturday.

1. अभी कविता क्या कर रही है? अभी कविता क्लास में जा रही है।

2. क्या कविता को मालूम है कि एक नयी फ़िल्म लगी है? जी नहीं, उसे मालूम नहीं है कि एक नयी फ़िल्म लगी है।

3. दीपक किस दिन और कितने बजे फ़िल्म देखने जाएगा? दीपक शनिवार की शाम को छै बजे फ़िल्म देखने जाएगा।

4. क्या दीपक कुछ दोस्तों के साथ फ़िल्म देखने के लिये जाएगा? जी हाँ, वह कुछ दोस्तों के साथ फ़िल्म देखने जाएगा।

5. क्या कविता को ऐसी फ़िल्में अच्छी लगती हैं? जी नहीं, कविता को ऐसी फ़िल्में इतनी अच्छी नहीं लगतीं।

6. क्या आपको हिन्दी फ़िल्में अच्छी लगती हैं? जी हाँ, मुझे हिन्दी फ़िल्में बहुत अच्छी लगती हैं। or जी नहीं, मुझे हिन्दी फ़िल्में अच्छी नहीं लगतीं।

7. क्या दीपक को यहाँ की चाय अच्छी लगती है? जी नहीं, दीपक को यहाँ की चाय अच्छी नहीं लगती।

8. आपको चाय पसंद है या कॉफ़ी? मुझे चाय पसंद है। or मुझको कॉफ़ी पसंद है। or मुझे चाय और कॉफ़ी दोनों पसंद हैं। or मुझे चाय और कॉफ़ी दोनों पसंद नहीं हैं।

9. क्या बारह बजे आपकी कक्षा है? जी नहीं, बारह बजे मेरी कक्षा नहीं है।

10. क्या तुम फ़िल्म देखने जाना चाहते हो? (चाहती हो) जी हाँ, मैं फ़िल्म देखने जाना चाहता हूँ। (चाहती हूँ)

Lesson 19

Activity 19.1

1. जी नहीं, मैं आ नहीं पाऊँगा। (पाऊँगी)
2. जी हाँ, मैं यह फ़िल्म देख चुका हूँ। (देख चुकी हूँ)
3. जी हाँ, मैं हिन्दी बोल भी सकता हूँ (बोल भी सकती हूँ)
4. यह काम कल दोपहर तक हो चुका होगा।
5. जी हाँ, वह गाड़ी चलाना सीख सकेगा।
6. जी नहीं, वह मुझे हिन्दुस्तान जाने के पैसे दे नहीं पाया।
7. जी नहीं, उस की पढ़ाई पूरी हो चुकी है।

Activity 19.2

मेट्रो में एक मुलाक़ात

कल एक बजे मैं मेट्रो से दिल्ली यूनिवर्सिटी जा रही थी। मेरे हाथ में तीन किताबें थीं। राजीव चौक के स्टेशन पर गाड़ी के दरवाज़े खुले और अचानक दीपक मेरे सामने आ खड़ा हो गया। बग़ल की कुर्सी ख़ाली थी। मैंने कहा कि "यहाँ बैठ जाओ।" फिर मैंने पूछा कि "क्या तुमने दिन का खाना खा लिया?" दीपक ने जवाब दिया कि "हाँ, मैं खाना खा चुका हूँ।" मैंने कहा कि "अगर तुमने खाना नहीं खाया होता तो मैं तुम्हें खाना खिला देती।" थोड़ी देर बाद उसने कहा "क्या तुम्हें अच्छी अंग्रेज़ी आती है?" मैंने कहा कि "हाँ, क्यों?" उसने मुझसे पूछा कि "क्या तुम मुझे अंग्रेज़ी सिखा सकती हो?" मैंने हँसकर कहा कि "हाँ, अगर तुम मुझसे अंग्रेज़ी सीख पाओगे तो मैं तुम्हें अंग्रेज़ी सिखा दूँगी।" दीपक दूसरी ओर देखकर मुस्करा दिया। फिर मैंने दीपक को एक अंग्रेज़ी की किताब दे दी और कहा कि "आज शाम को मेरे घर आना। मैं माँ से कह दूँगी कि तुम खाना खाने आ रहे हो।" उस के बाद बहाना बनाकर अचानक दीपक उठा और पुरानी दिल्ली स्टेशन पर उतर गया। मुझे ज़ोर की हँसी आ पड़ी।

A Meeting on the Metro

Yesterday at one o'clock I was going to Delhi University by the metro. I had three books in my hand. At Rajiv Chawk Station the doors opened and suddenly Deepak came and stood in front of me. The seat next to me was vacant. I said, "Sit down here." Then I asked, "Did you eat lunch?" Deepak answered, "Yes, I have already eaten." I said "I would have fed you if you hadn't eaten." After a little while he said, "Do you know English well?" I said, "Yes, why?" He asked, "Can you teach me English?" I laughed and said, "Yes, if you can learn English from me, I will teach you." Deepak looked in the other direction and smiled. Then I gave Deepak an English book and said, "Come to my home this evening. I will tell mom that you are coming for dinner." After this, Deepak made some excuse and suddenly got up and got down at Old Delhi Station. I burst into laughter.

Activity 19.3

1. मैं तुमसे लम्बा हूँ। (लम्बी)
2. तुम मेरे भाई से बड़े हो। (बड़ी)
3. हिन्दी अंग्रेज़ी से आसान है।
4. सातवाँ पाठ सब से मुश्किल होगा।
5. वह परिवार में सब से छोटी है।
6. वह फ़िल्म इस फ़िल्म से थोड़ी अच्छी है।
7. मुम्बई दिल्ली से बड़ा शहर है।
8. मुझे उन किताबों में से सब से मोटी किताब दे दीजिये।

Activity 19.4: Conversation

Kavita : Deepak, are you going back to Allahabad to celebrate Holi this year?

Deepak : I don't think that I can go. I have exams at that time.

Kavita : So come to our place to play. It will be so much fun. We celebrate all festivals with great gusto. My brother is coming from Australia in a few days as well. We have all of the things, the colors, the water pistols, etc. at home as well. All of the arrangements have already been made.

Deepak : I like the festival of Holi most of all.

Kavita : A few friends are also coming from college. You have old clothes, right?

Deepak : Where are my new clothes (I don't have any)? All of my clothes are old.

Kavita : That's true. So come in your oldest clothes that day. Remember, we play seriously. (we are not less than anyone in playing) We play for keeps. (having taken a stand we play)

Deepak : Okay, I will be ready. Don't (you) worry. I too am no slouch. (we are less than no one)

Kavita : Last year it took me a full week to get the color out.

Deepak : Do you (people) also make *gujhiya*?

Kavita : Of course! But be prepared (alert). My brother will eat all of the *gujhiyas*.

Deepak : Okay. So what time should I come to your house on Holi?

Kavita : Stay here overnight. My other friends will also stay over. We start playing very early in the morning, that's why.

1. इस साल क्या दीपक होली मनाने के लिये घर जा सकेगा? (जा पाएगा) जी नहीं, वह होली मनाने के लिये घर जा नहीं सकेगा। (जा नहीं पाएगा)

2. इस साल क्या आप होली मनाने हिन्दुस्तान जा सकेंगे? (जा सकेंगी) (पाना may also be used here.) जी हाँ, मैं हिन्दुस्तान होली मनाने जा सकूँगा। (जा सकूँगी) जी नहीं, मैं जा नहीं सकूँगा। (जा नहीं सकूँगी) (पाना may also be used here.)

3. क्या कविता का भाई ऑस्ट्रेलिया से होली मनाने को आएगा? जी हाँ, वह होली से कुछ दिन पहले आएगा।

4. क्या होली की सब तैयारियाँ हो चुकी हैं? जी हाँ, सब तैयारियाँ हो चुकी हैं।

5. क्या दीपक को होली का त्यौहार सब से अच्छा लगता है? जी हाँ, उसे होली का त्यौहार सब से अच्छा लगता है।

6. आपको कौन-सा त्यौहार सब से अच्छा लगता है? मुझे दीवाली का त्यौहार सब से अच्छा लगता है।

7. क्या लोग नये कपड़े पहनकर होली खेलते हैं? जी नहीं, वे पुराने कपड़े पहनकर खेलते हैं।

8. पिछले साल कविता को होली का रंग उतारने में कितने दिन लगे? पिछले साल रंग उतारने में कविता को एक पूरा हफ़्ता लगा।

9. क्या कविता का भाई सब गुझियाँ खा जाएगा? जी हाँ, वह सब गुझियाँ खा जाएगा।

Lesson 20

Activity 20.1

1. क्या आपको/तुम्हें चाय पीनी है?

2. मुझे/मुझको भारत जाकर हिन्दी सीखनी चाहिये।

3. कविता को अपने बारे में और बोलना चाहिये था।

4. हमें मई में अपना हिन्दी का इम्तहान देना पड़ेगा।

5. उसे यह किताब पढ़नी है।

6. Perhaps I will have to pay more rent next year.

7. The students should come to class only after doing their work.

8. No one should drink and drive.

9. At the end of this year everyone will just have to go to Lucknow.

10. You should have bought these books.

Activity 20.2

1. हमारी रेलगाड़ी छूटने वाली थी।

2. लंबेवाले लड़के को बुलाओ। (बुलाइये)

3. इस साल तीस हिन्दी सीखनेवाले हैं।

4. मैं सिगरेट पीनेवाला हूँ। (पीनेवाली हूँ) or मैं सिगरेट पीने को हूँ।

5. मैं सिगरेट पीनेवाला हूँ। (पीनेवाली हूँ)

6. मैं दिल्ली का रहनेवाला हूँ। (मैं दिल्ली की रहनेवाली हूँ।)

7. वह मांस खानेवाला है। or वह मांस खाने को है।

8. वह मांस खानेवाला है।

9. वे यह किताब पढ़नेवाले थे। or वे यह किताब पढ़ने को थे।

10. हरी जिल्द वाली किताब लाना। (लाइये/लाओ)
11. How many people are going to India at the end of this year?
12. It might be about to rain.
13. Give me your red sweater.
14. Tell the tea maker to make stronger tea than this.
15. I am about to go to university.

Activity 20.3: Conversation

Deepak : Hello Kavita. What brings you here?

Kavita : No reason. I was passing by here. So I thought I would meet you for five minutes. What are you doing right now?

Deepak : Nothing. I was about to have tea. Shall I have some tea made for you?

Kavita : Yes, I am craving tea.

Deepak : Shall I have strong or weak tea made?

Kavita : I like strong tea. Is Vrinda here?

Deepak : No. She had to go back to Allahabad just yesterday. She could only come for two weeks. Kavita, what are you going to do when your studies finish at the end of this month?

Kavita : It is my desire to go traveling and see the world before I begin studying medicine.

Deepak : Really. Where will you go?

Kavita : I must go and see my brother in Australia. I want to see what sort of place Australia is. If I like it then I might think about studying further there. Or perhaps I will make my way to America.

Deepak : Okay, the tea is ready. (made) Take (some). Don't you ever think about marriage?

Kavita : Oh, where do I have time for marriage? I want to do a lot in life. Work, travel, make my career, I have to do all of this.

Deepak : That's fine, but marriage also has its place. (is not such a bad thing in its place)

Kavita : Only if I find a good man, that is, a "life partner."

Deepak : You haven't found anyone yet?

Kavita : Perhaps there are one or two options. Oh, it's already five. I should go home.

Deepak : So quickly? You have just come.

Kavita : Yes, but really I will have to go. I came this way to do something for mom.

Deepak : Okay, I have brought a new DVD. If you want to watch a film, come over tomorrow.

Kavita : Okay, perhaps I will come tomorrow. What time?

Deepak : Come over any time in the evening. Okay, see you tomorrow.

1. क्या कविता जल्दी शादी करना चाहती है? जी नहीं, वह जल्दी शादी करना नहीं चाहती।
2. आप के ख़्याल में, क्या दीपक कविता से शादी करना चाहता है? जी हाँ, मेरे ख़्याल में दीपक कविता से शादी करना चाहता है।
3. क्या कविता को चाय पीनी है? जी हाँ, उसे चाय पीनी है।
4. क्या आपको/तुम्हें अभी चाय पीनी है? जी हाँ, मुझे/मुझको अभी चाय पीनी है।
5. आपको/तुमको तेज़वाली चाय पसंद है या हल्कीवाली? मुझे तेज़वाली चाय पसंद है।
6. पढ़ाई पूरी कर के क्या आप दुनिया देखना चाहते हैं? (देखना चाहती हैं) जी हाँ, पढ़ाई पूरी कर के मैं दुनिया देखना चाहता हूँ। (देखना चाहती हूँ)
7. पढ़ाई पूरी कर के क्या आप नौकरी करनेवाले हैं? (करनेवाली हैं) जी हाँ, पढ़ाई पूरी कर के मैं नौकरी करनेवाला हूँ। (करनेवाली हूँ)
8. क्या ज़िंदगी में आपको बहुत कुछ करना है? जी हाँ, ज़िंदगी में मुझको बहुत कुछ करना है।
9. आज रात को घर जाकर क्या तुम्हें खाना बनाना पड़ेगा? जी हाँ, आज रात को घर जाकर मुझे/मुझको खाना बनाना पड़ेगा। जी नहीं, आज रात को घर जाकर मुझे/मुझको खाना बनाना नहीं पड़ेगा।

Lesson 21

Activity 21.1

1. यह किताब पढ़ी गयी। This book was read.
2. हम सब लोगों के लिए टिकट ख़रीदे गये होंगे। Tickets must have been bought for all of us.
3. हारवर्ड यूनिवर्सिटी में हिन्दी सीखी जाती है। Hindi is learned at Harvard University.
4. उत्तर प्रदेश में हिन्दी बोली जाती है। Hindi is spoken in Uttar Pradesh.
5. चोर को गिरफ़्तार कर लिया गया। The thief was arrested.
6. एक नया क़ानून बनाया गया है। A new law has been made.
7. कहा जाता है कि पाकिस्तान से हिन्दुस्तान में ज़्यादा उर्दू बोली जाती है। It is said that more Urdu is spoken in India than in Pakistan.
8. शादी के लिये शानदार खाने की चीज़ें तैयार की गयीं। Splendid things to eat were prepared for the wedding.
9. अगर काम ठीक समय पर दे दिया जाता तो ... If the work has been given (handed in) on time, then...
10. यह सब खाना खाया गया। All of this food was eaten.

Activity 21.2

1. कल रात मुझसे सोया नहीं गया।
2. उससे यह किताब पढ़ी नहीं गयी।
3. उससे चावल बनाया नहीं जाएगा।
4. मुझसे यह फ़िल्म देखी नहीं जाती।
5. हमसे हिन्दुस्तान में पानी पिया नहीं जाता।
6. उनसे इतना तीखा खाना खाया नहीं जाता।
7. लखनऊ में छात्रों से रोज़ छै घंटे पढ़ा नहीं जाएगा।
8. संस्कृत इतनी मुश्किल है कि मुझसे सीखी नहीं जा रही है।

Activity 21.3: Conversation

Deepak : Hello Kavita. Why the hurry? Where are you going?
Kavita : Hey Deepak. I have to go to the pharmacy right now. It is quite a necessary task.
Deepak : Why? What happened? No one has become ill (have they)?
Kavita : Yes, my mother has become quite sick. Yesterday morning she couldn't get up. The doctor was also called. And then he said that she should have a blood test. The blood test was done yesterday. After that the doctor wrote a prescription and left. I am going to the pharmacy to get some medicine.
Deepak : Did the doctor tell (you) anything else?
Kavita : We were told that mom has a stomach infection. And she has quite a cough. She couldn't sleep all night.
Deepak : Was your mother taken to the hospital or not?
Kavita : No. She is at home at the moment. I hope that it won't be necessary to go.
Deepak : Can I help you (some)?
Kavita : Thank you. Not at the moment. Perhaps she will be better in one or two days.
Deepak : Okay. I will buy the medicine with you and then come to see her.
Kavita : Okay. The pharmacy is very close. It won't take even five minutes.

1. कौन बीमार हो गया है? कविता की माँ बीमार हो गयी है।
2. कविता को कहाँ जाना है? कविता को दवाख़ाने में दवा लेने जाना है।
3. क्या कविता को सड़क में दीपक मिलता है? जी हाँ, कविता को सड़क में दीपक मिलता है।
4. क्या डॉक्टर को बुलाया गया? जी हाँ, डॉक्टर को बुलाया गया।
5. क्या अभी आपको खाँसी हो रही है? जी नहीं, अभी मुझको खाँसी नहीं हो रही है।
6. क्या दीपक कविता की मदद करना चाहता है? जी हाँ, दीपक कविता की मदद करना चाहता है।

7. क्या कल रात को कविता की माँ से सोया नहीं गया? जी हाँ, कल रात को कविता की माँ से सोया नहीं गया।

8. क्या कविता की माँ को अस्पताल ले जाया गया? जी नहीं, कविता की माँ को अस्पताल ले जाया नहीं गया।

Lesson 22

Activity 22.1

1. हम हिन्दी सीखते रहेंगे। We will continue to learn Hindi.

2. तुम रोज़ कम से कम दो घंटे पढ़ाई किया करो। Study for at least two hours a day.

3. क्या आपसे भिखारियों की ओर देखते नहीं बनता? Can you not bear to look at beggars?

4. शायद वह हर साल भारत जाया करे। Perhaps he/she may go to India every year.

5. उस लड़की की तनख़्वाह बढ़ती ही जा रही थी। That girl's salary just kept increasing.

6. वे दोनों अभी अभी चले गये। They both just set off.

7. मुझे पैसे देते रहना। Continue to give me money.

8. ये लोग तस्वीरें खींचते जाते हैं। These people just go on snapping photos.

9. उसे दो दिन तक बिस्तर पर लेटे रहना पड़ा। He/she was forced to remain lying on the bed for two days.

10. हमारा दोस्त भाषण देता जाता है। Our friend just keeps on making a speech.

Activity 22.2

1. वह दिन भर पुस्तकालय में बैठा रहा।

2. मैं दिन भर हिन्दी पढ़ता रहता हूँ। (पढ़ती रहती हूँ)

3. हम हर समय भविष्य के बारे में सोचते रहते हैं।

4. तुम्हारी याद आती रहती है।

5. मैं दो घंटे तक बस में खड़ा रह गया। (खड़ी रह गयी)

Activity 22.3

1. अपने माँ-बाप के पास हर हफ़्ते जाया करो।

2. वे अक्सर फ़िल्में देखा करते हैं।

3. वह रोज़ एक किताब पढ़ा करती है।

4. इस कोने पर एक किताब की दुकान हुआ करती थी।

5. हम भारतयात्रा किया करेंगे।

Activity 22.4: Conversation

Kavita : Come Deepak. Sit (down). I was just waiting for you. What will you drink? Cold coffee, coffee, milk shake, tea?

Deepak : Only tea.

Kavita : Just tea? I am paying. Have (take) something more.

Deepak : Tea will be enough. I don't feel like drinking anything else.

Kavita : Okay, *baba*. As you wish. What are you thinking about today?

Deepak : What can I tell (you)? Do you ever think how quickly our lives are changing?

Kavita : Yes, I think about this constantly. The pace of life is getting faster and faster. Now who doesn't have a cell phone? There are so many new cars coming onto the roads every day. Day by day the face of (map of) Delhi is changing. Now I can't even recognize the city of Delhi.

Deepak : Yes. It now seems that the cycle of change will just continue to turn. Now the metro is also running. (has begun) People have so much wealth. Nevertheless, people still run after money. And now so many things are available in the stores.

Kavita : Some people have got a lot of money now, but not all people. And the prices of things just continue to increase.

Deepak : This is true. But what can (should) be done? Some people's lives are getting better and some people's lives are becoming more difficult.

Kavita : It would not be wrong to say that here some things have become much better and some have gotten much worse. (If it may be said that … this would not be wrong)

Deepak : But overall (having added the total) I think that here progress is now continuing to take place.

Kavita : Perhaps. Let's see in ten years. (after ten years it will be seen)

1. कविता और दीपक कहाँ मिलते हैं? कविता और दीपक कैफ़े में मिलते हैं।

2. क्या कविता दीपक का इंतज़ार कर रही थी? जी हाँ, कविता दीपक का इंतज़ार कर रही थी।

3. क्या दीपक सिर्फ़ चाय पीना चाहता है? जी हाँ, दीपक सिर्फ़ चाय पीना चाहता है।

4. दिल्ली में क्या ज़िंदगी बदलती जा रही है? जी हाँ, दिल्ली में ज़िंदगी बदलती जा रही है।

5. अब क्या दुकानों में बहुत चीज़ें मिलने लगी हैं? जी हाँ, अब दुकानों में बहुत चीज़ें मिलने लगी हैं।

6. क्या कविता बदलाव के बारे में सोचती रहती है? जी हाँ, कविता बदलाव के बारे में सोचती रहती है।

7. क्या चीज़ों के दाम बढ़ते जा रहे हैं? जी हाँ, चीज़ों के दाम बढ़ते जा रहे हैं।

8. क्या अब सब लोगों के पास बहुत दौलत है? जी नहीं, सब लोगों के पास बहुत दौलत नहीं है।

9. क्या दीपक सोचता है कि दिल्ली में तरक़्क़ी होती जा रही है? जी हाँ, दीपक सोचता है कि दिल्ली में तरक़्क़ी होती जा रही है।

Lesson 23

Activity 23.1

1. जो क़मीज़ आपने पहन रखी* है वह मुझे बहुत पसंद है। I really like the shirt you are wearing.

   * Note, there is another written form of the perfective participle of the verb रखना, रक्खा, which corresponds to the standard pronunciation.

2. जहाँ भी आप जायें मैं भी वहीं जाऊँगी। I (f) will go wherever you may go.

3. जो भी तुम्हें चाहिये वे आपको दे देंगे। They/he will give you whatever you want.

4. जिन छात्रों ने हिन्दी पढ़ी वे सब साल के अंत में भारत गये। All of the students who studied Hindi went to India at the end of the year.

5. तभी आप का काम हो पाएगा जब आप मन लगाकर पढ़ाई करेंगे। (करेंगी) You will succeed (your work will be able to happen) only when you apply your heart/mind and study.

6. जितना काम तुम कर सकते हो, उतना ही करो। Do as much work as you are able to.

Activity 23.2

1. We children lived with mom for as long as she worked in America.

2. How will they know that we are about to get married until this letter is sent?

3. How will you learn to drive a car until you practice driving?

4. This work will not get done until you help me.

5. Stay seated here until I come.

6. जब तक मैं न कहूँ तब तक काम करते रहो। (करती रहो)

7. जब तक यह हो जाएगा तब तक वे जा चुके होंगे।

8. जब तक मैं काम ख़त्म कर सका तब तक उसके पास मेरे लिये समय नहीं रह गया था।

9. जब तक आप पहाड़ों में जाएँगे तब तक बर्फ़ पिघल जाएगी।

10. जब तक यह न हो तब तक मैं जा नहीं सकूँगा। (सकूँगी)

Activity 23.3: Conversation

Kavita   : Deepak, why are you so late? I have been waiting for half an hour. My coffee has become cold.
Deepak : Forgive me, Kavita. I lost a book. I was searching for it.
Kavita   : Which book?
Deepak : The book I told you about. I had bought it for you.
Kavita   : For me? Really? The book with the red cover? The one about Bollywood cinema?
Deepak : Yes, that one. I took it into the library. And now I can't find it anywhere.
Kavita   : Was anyone else sitting near you in the library?
Deepak : No. It is a very empty place.
Kavita   : Were you with anyone else when you went into the library?
Deepak : No. I went alone. Even you weren't with me.
Kavita   : Were you holding your stuff in the library like you are holding it at the moment?
Deepak : Yes, why? I won't find peace until I find this book.
Kavita   : Deepak, you must have looked in your bag, right?
Deepak : Kavita, do you think I am an idiot? How could it be in the bag?
Kavita   : Whatever. Just take a look (once). Who knows, perhaps you may find it.
Deepak : Oh no. The book is in the bag. I am so embarrassed.
Kavita   : No matter. That often happens to (with) me. Okay, drink some tea.

1. दीपक को देर क्यों हुई? दीपक को देर हुई क्योंकि उसकी एक किताब खो गयी थी।

2. कविता कब से इंतज़ार कर रही थी? कविता आधे घंटे से इंतज़ार कर रही थी।

3. दीपक ने किसके लिए किताब ख़रीदी थी? दीपक ने कविता के लिए किताब ख़रीदी थी।

4. दीपक किताब को कहाँ ले गया था? दीपक किताब को लाइब्रेरी में ले गया था।

5. क्या दीपक के साथ कोई और लाइब्रेरी में बैठा था? जी नहीं, दीपक के साथ कोई और लाइब्रेरी में नहीं बैठा था।

6. जब तक किताब न मिलेगी क्या तब तक दीपक को चैन मिलेगा? जी नहीं, जब तक किताब न मिलेगी तब तक दीपक को चैन नहीं मिलेगा।

7. क्या दीपक ने बस्ते में देखा होगा? जी नहीं, दीपक ने बस्ते में नहीं देखा होगा।

8. क्या किताब दीपक के बस्ते में है? जी हाँ, किताब दीपक के बस्ते में है।

9. क्या कविता सोचती है कि दीपक बेवकूफ़ है? जी नहीं, कविता नहीं सोचती कि दीपक बेवकूफ़ है।

Lesson 24

Activity 24.1

1. A woman was visible coming along.
2. I woke up my sleeping brother.
3. Don't swim in flowing water.
4. Forever-changing ideas are never firm/fixed.
5. Shut up the speaking girl.
6. मेज़ पर पड़ी (हुई) क़लम मेरी है।
7. दीवार पर लगी (हुई) तस्वीर बहुत सुन्दर (ख़ूबसूरत) है।
8. मिले (हुए) पैसे मत गँवाओ। (गँवाइये/गँवाना)
9. खुला (हुआ) दरवाज़ा बंद करो। (कीजिये)
10. वह आधी खायी (हुई) रोटी मत खाओ। (खाइए/खाना)

Activity 24.2

1. एक बार चलते-चलते दीपक ने अपनी जेब में हाथ डाला। Once, while walking, Deepak put his hand in his pocket.
2. कल विश्वविद्यालय जाते-समय वह अपनी लिखी एक चिट्ठी कविता को देना चाहता था। Yesterday when he was going to university, he wanted to give Kavita a letter he had written.
3. पर कविता से मिलते-वक़्त उसे लगा कि चिट्ठी खो गयी होगी। But when he met Kavita, it seemed as if the letter must have become lost.
4. पर अभी जेब में हाथ डालते ही उसने देखा कि चिट्ठी तो कोट की जेब में ही पड़ी थी। But right now, as soon as he put his hand in his pocket, he saw that the letter was actually in the pocket of his coat.
5. अब जब कविता मिलेगी तो उसे वह हँसते हुए यह चिट्ठी दे देगा। Now, when he runs into Kavita, he will give her the letter laughing.
6. अपनी किताबें सँभालते हुए वह और उसकी नयी दोस्त पुस्तकालय से बाहर निकले। Taking (care of) his own books, he left the library with his new friend.
7. होरी को उपवास करते हुए कई दिन हो गए थे। Hori had been fasting for several days.
8. भूख लगते ही मनपसंद खाना उसके सामने आ जाता था। As soon as he/she became hungry, his/her favorite foods were placed in front of him/her.
9. दीपक को कविता की याद आने लगी जिसे कल वह रोते हुए छोड़ आया था। Deepak began to think of Kavita, whom he had left crying yesterday.
10. बच्चों के सोते समय ही वह अपनी पढ़ाई पूरी कर पाती थी। She was only able to complete her studies when the children were sleeping.
11. आज भी जब खाना न मिला तो मन ही मन तरह-तरह के पकवानों का स्वाद लेते हुए वह सो गया। When he didn't get food to eat again today, then he slept thinking of the taste of all manner of rich foods.

Activity 24.3

1. आपको यह किताब पढ़ते हुए कितने दिन हुए हैं?
2. उसे भारत में रहते हुए दो साल हो गये हैं।
3. उन्हें/उनको फ़ोन में बातचीत करते हुए चार घंटे हुए थे।
4. उस समय हमें किताबें बेचते (हुए) बाईस साल हो गये थे।
5. आपको हिन्दी सीखते हुए कितने साल हुए हैं?
6. मुझको हिन्दी सीखते हुए नौ महीने हुए हैं।
7. It has been two hours since they spoke.
8. It has been nine months since I learned Hindi.
9. It has been two years since he/she went to India.
10. How long has it been since you learned Hindi?
11. At that time it was just a few days since we had sold our house.
12. How many days has it been since you read this book?

Activity 24.4: Conversation

Deepak : Kavita, for how many years have you been living in Delhi?
Kavita : I have been living here for two years. And you?
Deepak : I have been here for two years as well. How long is it since your brother who lives in Australia has been to India?
Kavita : It has been six months since he has been here. I think of him a lot when I write letters to him.
Deepak : Okay, what were you doing yesterday when I was studying in the library?
Kavita : I must have been taking a book to my friend's house at the time. Why?
Deepak : I saw you as I was coming out of the library and thought to myself that I should call out to you. But I stopped and you disappeared down some lane.

Kavita : I keep saying that you should not be shy. Even though (while) you know that I like being with you, you are still nervous.

Deepak : It is not like that. I didn't want to go home without talking to you.

Kavita : If I had been in your shoes (place), I would not have been able to stay without meeting with you. Okay, I should go home now. It will be night by the time I get home.

Deepak : Kavita, do you…

Kavita : What Deepak? What do you want to say? Why did you stop (while saying)? What is it?

Deepak : Nothing. Will you have coffee with me before going home?

Kavita : Okay. But quickly, because I have to go out at night.

Deepak : [to himself] Will I be able to summon the courage to tell her how I feel in the café?

1. कविता को दिल्ली में रहते (हुए) कितने साल हुए हैं? कविता को दिल्ली में रहते (हुए) दो साल हुए हैं।

2. आपको यहाँ रहते (हुए) कितने साल हुए हैं? मुझे यहाँ रहते (हुए) एक साल हुआ है। (दो साल हुए हैं)

3. दीपक को दिल्ली में रहते (हुए) कितने साल हुए हैं? दीपक को भी दिल्ली में रहते (हुए) दो साल हुए हैं।

4. कविता के भाई को भारत आये हुए कितने दिन हुए हैं? कविता के भाई को भारत आये (हुए) छै महीने हुए हैं।

5. आपको हिन्दुस्तान गये (हुए) कितने दिन हुए हैं? मुझको हिन्दुस्तान गये (हुए) एक साल हुआ है। (दो साल हुए हैं)

6. दीपक के पुस्तकालय में पढ़ते-समय कविता कहाँ जा रही होगी? दीपक के पुस्तकालय में पढ़ते-समय कविता अपने दोस्त के घर जा रही होगी।

7. क्या दीपक को चाहिये था कि वह कविता को पुकारता? जी हाँ, दीपक को कविता को पुकारना चाहिये था।

8. क्या आज रात कविता को बाहर जाना है? जी हाँ, आज रात को कविता को बाहर जाना है।

9. क्या आज रात को तुम्हें बाहर जाना है? जी हाँ, आज रात को मुझे बाहर जाना है। or जी नहीं, आज रात को मुझे बाहर जाना नहीं है।

10. क्या दीपक को अपने मन की बात कविता को बतानी चाहिये? जी हाँ, दीपक को अपने मन की बात कविता को बतानी चाहिये।